MS-EX(

FOR WINDOW;

Benno Brudermans

MS-EXCEL 4.0
FOR WINDOWS

PRISMA
COMPUTER
COURSE

Prisma Computer Courses first published in Great Britain 1992 by

McCarta Ltd
15 Highbury Place
London N5 1QP

Translation: Claire Singleton
Production: LINE UP text productions

© Rowohlt Taschenbuch Verlag GmbH, Reinbek bei Hamburg
For the English translation
© 1992 Uitgeverij Het Spectrum B.V., Utrecht

ISBN 1 85365 350 0

British Library Cataloguing-in-Publication Data.
A catalogue record for this book is available from the British Library.

Contents

Foreword

The most important personal computer (PC) application, apart from word processing, is calculation. Since the launch in 1979 of VISICALC (the first spreadsheet program), many others have been marketed as individual programs or as part of a so-called integrated package. The programs were adapted both quantitatively and qualitatively to the continually increasing operating speed of computer hardware.

EXCEL sets a new standard in spreadsheet programs. Firstly, EXCEL was developed for the Apple MacIntosh, but Microsoft soon decided to develop a version for PCs, and a version for the OS/2 PRESENTATION MANAGER has also since been produced. At first sight, EXCEL seems no different from many other spreadsheet programs, but EXCEL has the advantage over other spreadsheets in that the program runs under WINDOWS, the powerful graphic user interface. This means that EXCEL can make full use of all the possibilities offered by this interface, such as WYSIWYG (What You See Is What You Get), mouse control, excellent output quality and many data exchange possibilities.

This book is aimed particularly at new users. Examples of problems are used to explain the EXCEL program's most important functions in a clear and systematic way. No previous knowledge is required. The intention is that the examples are tested directly on the computer. There are many exercises to help broaden your knowledge. All the examples have been designed and tested in EXCEL 4.0 running under WINDOWS 3.1.

1 Basic skills for working with EXCEL

1.1 The program

The EXCEL program has three basic components - worksheets, charts and databases.

Worksheets

A worksheet, the heart of EXCEL, is used for processing and storing text and number values. These values can be linked together using many arithmetical and logical operators. If a value or a parameter changes in a worksheet, you only have to correct this value to obtain the new result directly. The values which remain unchanged do not have to be entered again. This means that worksheets are highly suited to a wide variety of calculations. EXCEL makes it possible to work with several worksheets simultaneously, each of which can be displayed in a separate window on the screen and can also be linked to the others.

Charts

Nowadays statistical figures are often displayed in the form of charts and diagrams, which give a better overview. EXCEL offers the possibility of incorporating into a chart some or all of the material contained in a worksheet. You can choose from various types of charts and diagrams (area charts, bar and column charts, pie charts, line charts, radar charts, XY charts or a combination of these).

Databases

It is possible to define parts of a worksheet or even entire worksheets as a database range. Large quantities of data can be entered into a database range and can then be structured, arranged and retrieved depending on given criteria.

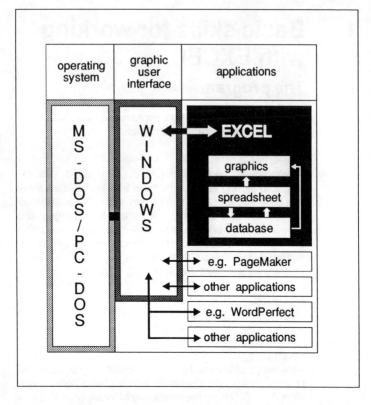

EXCEL's special features include:

Consistent use of the WINDOWS graphic user interface
A window is opened for every loaded or newly created worksheet. It is possible to display several windows of differing sizes next to each other, overlaid or on top of each other. The number of windows which can be simultaneously displayed depends on the amount of available RAM. You can enlarge and reduce windows, as well as move them around the screen. Every window can in turn be divided into a maximum of four panes. The WINDOWS graphic user interface offers a wide range of fonts in varying sizes. Even the cells of a work-

sheet can be widened and lengthened elastically. It is also possible for data to be exchanged between individual windows.

Powerful print function

It is possible to produce excellent quality print-outs of worksheets, both horizontally and vertically. Depending on the printer you have installed, EXCEL offers a wide variety of fonts for use in worksheets and charts as desired. You can position headers and footers, and use lines, frames and patterns to emphasise particular data. Print previewing is particularly useful, enabling a worksheet or chart to be displayed page by page exactly as it will be printed.

Full mouse control

All EXCEL menus, commands and functions can be operated either by using the keyboard or the mouse. In both cases, program operation is quick and easy to learn. Appendix A (at the back of the book) gives a summary of the key combinations for operating EXCEL using the keyboard.

Powerful, easy-to-use macrolanguage

EXCEL makes it possible to store key strokes and processing procedures in macros, separate from the worksheet. You can also use this macrolanguage to write programs yourself. Powerful commands are available, for example for conditional jumps, controlling a loop or calling up subroutines. It is also possible to create message and dialog boxes, as well as pull-down menus with user-defined commands. In addition to these command macros, EXCEL also has function macros which you can use to create your own functions.

Data exchange

EXCEL can load worksheets and macros made in MULTIPLAN or LOTUS 1-2-3, and convert them into EXCEL format. Furthermore, EXCEL can also exchange data with other programs running under WINDOWS.

The Help system
EXCEL offers no fewer than four different help functions:

a) Using *F1* you can call up *context-oriented help* at any time.

b) The *Help Index*, containing a summary of topics and general information, is always available via the *Help* menu.

c) Using the *Tutorial*, you will soon have mastered the basic skills.

d) *Help for MULTIPLAN and LOTUS 1-2-3 users*. If you enter a MULTIPLAN or LOTUS 1-2-3 function, this help function shows the EXCEL equivalent.

1.2 System requirements

A powerful program like EXCEL has high hardware and software requirements. In order to use EXCEL, you will need the following:

■ a personal computer (PC) with an i80286, i80386 or i80486 processor
■ 2 MB RAM
■ a minimum of 6 MB available harddisk capacity
■ a VGA, EGA or HERCULES screen and graphics card
■ a mouse (optional)
■ operating system MS-DOS version 3.1 or more recent
■ the WINDOWS graphic user interface, version 3.0 or more recent.

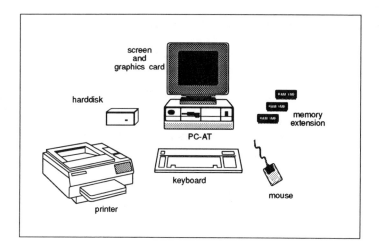

This book makes the following assumptions (although it is of course possible to run EXCEL on other configurations):

■ EXCEL is installed on harddisk C: in the EXCEL directory.
■ There is a subdirectory called C:\EXCEL\EXERCISE.
■ The computer has a 5.25 inch disk drive A: and a 3.5 inch disk drive B:.
■ A mouse is connected and a PostScript laser printer is used for printing.

1.3   Installation

In order to use EXCEL, you must first install it on your computer's harddisk.

However, EXCEL can only run under WINDOWS, which is why this user interface has to be installed first, if that has not already taken place.

Follow these instructions to install WINDOWS:

1   Insert the first program diskette in drive A: or B:.

2   Start the installation program by typing the command
    'a:\setup' or 'b:\setup', as appropriate.

3   Follow the installation program instructions.

When you have specified a directory for installing WIN-
DOWS, SETUP requests information about:

a) the computer

b) the screen (HERCULES, EGA, VGA, monochrome
   or colour)

c) the mouse

d) the keyboard

e) the keyboard layout

f) the language

g) the network (if any).

When you have answered these questions, the installation program makes the directory you have indicated on
your harddisk and copies the necessary files to it. At the
right time, SETUP will ask you to insert the next diskette
in the drive. During installation you have the chance to
select a printer. Follow the instructions given by
SETUP.

If you make a mistake during installation, you can abort
SETUP by pressing the Ctrl-X key combination, and
restart the installation program.

Once WINDOWS is installed, you can install EXCEL.
To do this, follow the instructions below:

1   Start WINDOWS by typing the command 'win' and
    confirm with Enter. You may first have to make active

the drive and directory where you have stored WIN-DOWS.

2 Wait for the Program Manager window to appear on the screen.

3 Open the *File* menu using the mouse, or using key combination Alt-F.

4 Select the *Run* option using the mouse, the arrow keys and Enter, or by typing the letter R.

5 Start the installation program by typing 'a:setup' or 'b:setup', as appropriate, and confirm by pressing Enter.

6 Enter the name of the directory where EXCEL is to be installed. Confirm the standard setup 'C:\EXCEL'.

7 Select 'Complete Installation'.

EXCEL will now be installed in the directory you have indicated. During installation, follow the instructions given by SETUP. Once all the files have been copied, SETUP creates a group window for EXCEL. Here, you will find the icons which you will use to start EXCEL and its related help programs.

1.4   The WINDOWS user interface

1.4.1   Starting WINDOWS

Before using EXCEL, you must first start the WIN-DOWS program. As mentioned above, this is done using the command 'win', followed by Enter. If you have not included the WINDOWS directory in the DOS path, you will first have to activate the relevant drive and directory, and then give the 'win' command. Once the logo has disappeared from the screen, the WINDOWS Program Manager window appears:

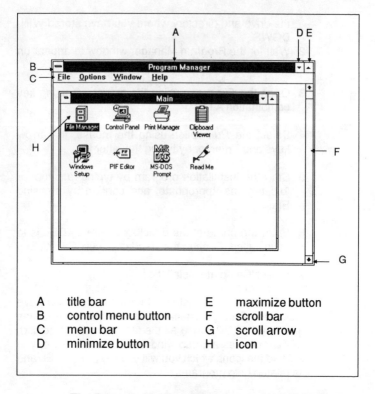

A	title bar	E	maximize button
B	control menu button	F	scroll bar
C	menu bar	G	scroll arrow
D	minimize button	H	icon

The Program Manager is the heart of WINDOWS. This is where you start programs like EXCEL, and you return to it when you exit a program.

1.4.2   WINDOWS basic skills

We will now introduce you to WINDOWS and the way this interface operates, using the Program Manager window. The method you will learn here applies to all WINDOWS applications, including EXCEL.

Working with windows
A window has a narrow frame. Position the mouse pointer to the left or right of the frame. You will see that

the mouse pointer changes into a double arrow. If you press the left mouse button and hold it down, the colour of the frame changes. You can now make the window wider or narrower by moving the mouse.

By positioning the mouse pointer on the top or bottom of the frame, you can change the height of the window. To change the height and width of a window simultaneously, move the mouse pointer to one of the four corners of the frame.

The title bar, showing the name of the window, is located under the frame's upper border. Position the mouse pointer on the name in the title bar, then press and hold down the left mouse button. You can now move the window around the screen, without altering its size.

You will notice two buttons on the right of the title bar. The right-hand button, with the arrow pointing upwards, is the *maximize button.* If you click on it, the window will become full-screen size and the button changes to a double arrow. If you click on the button again, the window is restored to its original size.

The button next to it, with the arrow pointing downwards, is the *minimize button.* If you click on it, you will shrink the window to an *icon.* If you double-click on the icon, the window is restored. Finally, return the window to full-screen size.

Using these processing methods, you can arrange several differently-sized windows on your screen. However, you can only work in one window at a time. This is known as the current window and it has a shaded title bar.

Groups
All programs in the Program Manager are contained in *groups.* These groups can be compared to files which can hold up to 40 programs. Each group has its own window within the Program Manager. When WINDOWS

has been installed, only the Main window is open. The other groups made during installation have been reduced to icons at the bottom of the screen. These groups can be opened by clicking on them. Try this out on the Accessories group.

We should distinguish here between *application windows*, such as the Program Manager, and *group windows*, such as the Main Group window. In group windows, programs are displayed as icons, with the name of the program given underneath. In contrast to an application window, a group window has no menu bar.

To start a particular program, double-click on the relevant icon. Try this out on the Clock program in the Accessories group. An application window appears on your screen, containing an analogue clock. To return to the Program Manager, simply click anywhere inside the workspace of that window. The clock disappears behind the Program Manager.

Even if one application window is overlaid on another, you can switch from one to the other. To do this, use the *control menu button*, the small rectangle in the top left-hand corner of the window. Clicking on this button opens the *Control Menu*; the command *Switch To* calls up the Task List window. Here you will find a list of all loaded programs. Using the mouse, select the required program and click on the *Switch To* button to start it.

To end a program, select the *Close* command from the *Control Menu*. You are already familiar with the other commands in the *Control menu*. Take time to experiment with the various possible ways of starting, shrinking and ending programs.

Menus
Under the title bar, you will see the *menu bar*, containing the WINDOWS menus. Every application window has its own menus. Only the Control menu is the same in every window. The following menus can be found in the Program Manager:

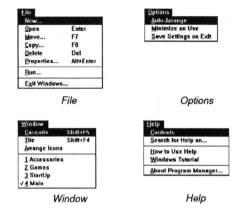

File   *Options*

Window   *Help*

To open a menu, place the mouse pointer on the name of the menu and press the left mouse button. The menu will then be displayed underneath the name. The first command in the menu is highlighted. Sometimes commands are shown in grey lettering, which indicates that they are not available at the moment.

If you have accidentally opened the wrong menu, you can close it by clicking outside the relevant menu. Practise by opening the *Window* menu. This menu enables you to arrange windows on the screen. Click on the *Cascade* command. All open groups will now be displayed overlapping. Now select *Tile*. The Program Manager window no longer fills the screen.

You will see a horizontal and a vertical *scroll bar* in the window. You can use this bar to move the window's contents vertically or horizontally.

■ Clicking on one of the two scroll arrows moves the window's contents step-by-step.
■ Dragging the box along the scroll bar moves the window's contents continuously.
■ Clicking on the scroll bar moves the window's contents in stages.

Dialog boxes
Extra information is required to process certain commands. These commands can be recognised by the three dots (...) called ellipsis after the name. If you select this type of command, a dialog box appears on the screen, allowing you to enter a file name, for example, or change settings.

A dialog box can contain the following elements:

- **a command button:** a rectangular area used to start an action or to lead to other options
- **a text box:** a rectangular box where you can type text or numbers
- **a list box:** a list from which a choice can be made. The list can be extended using the scroll arrows
- **a drop-down list box:** when you select the arrow in the square at the right of the list, the available choices appear
- **an option button:** a rounded box, usually used to choose from several options, where activating one option excludes another
- **a check box:** a square area used to activate or deactivate an option. Several check boxes can be active at the same time.

Exercise

1) Open the *File* menu.

2) Select the *New* command.

3) Activate *Program Group*.

4) Click on *OK*.

5) In the *Description* text box, type 'New group'.

6) Click on *OK*.
   You have now made a new group where you can place your own programs.

Throughout this book, you will become familiar with many other dialog boxes.

1.4.3   Starting applications under WINDOWS

Applications can be started up in various ways under WINDOWS. We shall now demonstrate this using EXCEL.

Starting from the Program Manager

1   Start WINDOWS as described in section 1.4.1.

2   In the Program Manager, double-click on the Micro-soft EXCEL icon.

Starting WINDOWS and an application at the same time

If the WINDOWS directory and the directory for the ap-plication you wish to start are in the DOS path, you can start WINDOWS and the relevant application at the same time. For EXCEL, for example, give the command 'win excel' and then press Enter. When WINDOWS has been started up, EXCEL is automatically activated.

1.4.4   Exiting WINDOWS

There are also several ways of exiting WINDOWS, which are all implemented from the Program Manager:

■ using the command *Exit Windows* from the *File* menu
■ using the command *Close* from the control menu
■ by double-clicking on the system box
■ using the key combination Alt-F4.

In all cases, this dialog box appears on the screen:

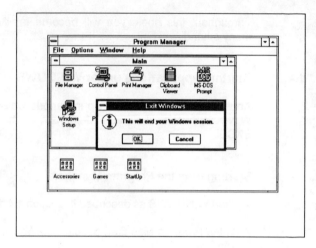

Use *OK* to exit WINDOWS, and *Cancel* to go back to
the Program Manager. If you activate *Save Settings on
Exit* from the *Options* menu, the changes you have
made to the Program Manager will be stored for future
use when you start WINDOWS again.

1.5   Using the EXCEL help system

**EXCEL provides extensive user-support which of-
fers:**

■ help with the selected command
■ help with the active dialog box
■ help with a message
■ a help index and a tutorial program.

1.5.1   The Help system

Excel's Help window
EXCEL offers help in a special window. The structure of
this window is no different from that of other WINDOWS
windows (see section 1.4):

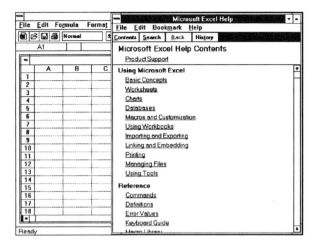

Under the menu bar you will see the buttons which control the Help system. The *Contents* option calls up a list of general topics about which information is available. The *Back* button takes you back to the previous help screen. With the *History* button you can return to any of the last 50 Help topics you have viewed since starting EXCEL.

To search for a specific item, select the *Search* button. You will see the following dialog box:

In the *Search* text box, type the item you wish to search for or click on one of the items in the list. Then click on

the *Show Topics* button. A list of topics found appears
at the bottom of the dialog box. You can choose from
them and then click on the *Go To* button to call up the
required information.

Some items of the help text are underlined. If you click
on one of them, a new help text appears containing detailed information about the relevant topic. Other items
in the help text are underlined with a dotted line. If you
click on one of them, you will obtain information about
the relevant item in a separate window.

Activating the help system
There are various ways of calling up the help system:

■ Using *F1* you can consult the help text for the command you have chosen, the current dialog box or the
  message shown on the screen. When you press F1,
  the help window appears on the screen with the required information.
■ It is also possible to call up the help screen before
  you start a command. This is done using *Shift-F1*.
  The mouse pointer changes into a question mark.
  You will see a help text for the next command you
  select.
■ Using the *Contents* command from the *Help* menu.

1.5.2   Help for LOTUS 1-2-3 and MULTIPLAN users

If you have already used LOTUS 1-2-3 or MULTIPLAN,
you can activate the EXCEL versions of LOTUS 1-2-3
or MULTIPLAN functions using the relevant commands
from the Help menu. Type the abbreviated form of the
name of the MULTIPLAN function in the dialog box on
your screen. Then click on the *OK* button to request information about the corresponding EXCEL function.
The help function for LOTUS 1-2-3 is more extensive.
Select a topic and activate one of the options to receive
more advice.

1.5.3 Introducing Microsoft Excel

This short Help program deals with three topics: *The Basics*, *What's New* and *For Lotus 1-2-3 Users*. Select these in turn to gain an outline of the possibilities of Excel.

1.5.4 Learning Microsoft Excel

Using the tutorial, a new user can quickly gain the required basic knowledge for working with EXCEL. The tutorial covers the following subjects:

- Introduction
- Worksheets
- Charts
- Databases
- Macros
- Toolbars

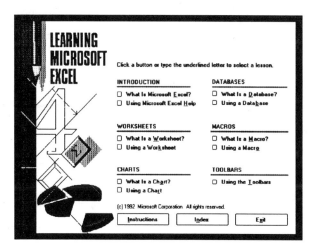

You can interrupt the tutorial at any time and pick it up again where you stopped the previous time.

1.5.5   Shortcut menus

Wherever you are working, whether in a worksheet or in a chart, you can always activate a *Shortcut* menu by pressing the right-hand mouse button. This Shortcut menu provides a concise list of available options for the task in hand.

1.6   Questions

1) What are the three main components of the EXCEL program?
   a) _____
   b) _____
   c) _____

2) Which key is used to request context-related help?
   _____
   _____

3) Where on the screen is the control menu? _____
   _____
   _____

4) How would you do the following?
   a) Start EXCEL directly from DOS: _____
   _____

   b) Exit WINDOWS: _____

   c) Reduce an application window to an icon: _____
   _____

5) What are the possible components of a dialog box?
   a) _____
   b) _____
   c) _____
   d) _____
   e) _____
   f) _____

1.7 Answers

1) What are the three main components of the EXCEL program?
   a) Worksheets
   b) Charts
   c) Databases

2) Which key is used to request context-related help?
   F1

3) Where on the screen is the control menu?
   To the left of the title bar.

4) How would you do the following?
   a) Start EXCEL directly from DOS:
      Using the 'win excel' command, possibly from the WINDOWS program directory.
   b) Exit WINDOWS:
      By double-clicking on the control box and clicking on the OK button in the dialog box which appears on the screen.
   c) Reduce an application window to an icon:
      By clicking on the minimize button at the top right of the title bar.

5 What are the possible components of a dialog box?
   a) *Command buttons*
   b) Text boxes
   c) *List boxes*
   d) Drop-down list boxes
   e) *Option buttons*
   f) Check boxes

2   Worksheets

2.1   The structure of a worksheet

Spreadsheet programs are used primarily for economic and administrative applications. However, they are gaining in popularity in science, technology and in the home.

A spreadsheet, which is also known as a worksheet, consists of **cells** arranged in **rows** and **columns**. These cells contain numbers, text or formulas. The formulas make it possible to combine numbers in many different ways using arithmetical operations.

It is possible to recalculate the entire worksheet if the contents of one or more cells change. This has the following advantages:

- Arithmetical processes are faster.
- Values can be corrected rapidly and simply.
- Worksheets with different values can be used for solving conditional questions.

An EXCEL worksheet consists of a maximum of **256** columns and **16,384** rows, making a total of **4,194,304** cells. However, only part of the worksheet is visible on the screen. Imagine the screen as a magnifying glass which you can move around the worksheet using the mouse and the scroll bars to reveal a particular section.

The **columns** are labelled with capital letters, from **A** to **IV** (A, B, ... Z; AA, AB, ... AZ; BA, BB ... BZ; ...; IA, IB ... IV). EXCEL also enables columns to be labelled with digits from 1 to 156 inclusive. The **column headers** are the cells at the top of the column. The **row headers** are on the left at the beginning of each row. The rows are numbered from 1 to 16,384 inclusive. It is not possible to use letters to label rows.

2.2 The EXCEL application window

EXCEL opens up by displaying the **EXCEL application window**:

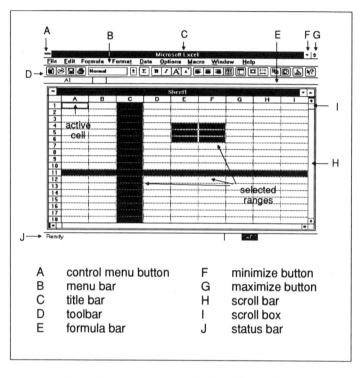

A	control menu button	F	minimize button
B	menu bar	G	maximize button
C	title bar	H	scroll bar
D	toolbar	I	scroll box
E	formula bar	J	status bar

There is an obvious similarity with the Program Manager window. At the top of the window you will see the **title bar** and under it the **menu bar**, containing the EXCEL menus. Under that you will see a new element - the **toolbar**. This offers a wide range of processing possibilities. Under the toolbar is a row containing the **reference area** and the **formula bar**. The **status bar** at the bottom of the screen provides information about the selected command and the current status of the workspace.

2.3   The worksheet window

Between the formula bar and the status bar is the actual
workspace where the EXCEL worksheets are displayed
as a **worksheet window**. When you start EXCEL, you
will automatically be presented an empty worksheet
window. Inside the workspace, you can also open several worksheet windows containing different fragments
of the same worksheet or different worksheets. We will
come back to this in more detail later.

2.3.1   Components

Have another look at the worksheet window in the previous illustration. EXCEL has automatically given the
worksheet the name 'Sheet1'. You can change this
name when you save the updated worksheet. You can
change the size of the worksheet using the techniques
described earlier, such as moving the window frame or
clicking on the maximize button. Using the vertical and
horizontal scroll bars, you can look up any desired part
of the worksheet.

Gridlines separate the individual cells in the worksheet.
The letters in the column headings and the digits in the
row headings combine to form a set of coordinates
which can be used to determine the position of each
cell. So, for example, the coordinates A1 refer to the
marked cell in row 1 of column A. These coordinates
are known as **references.** Using the **alphanumeric reference format** the column letter is given first, followed
by the row number (e.g. B12). The **numeric reference
format** is exactly the other way round: the row reference is followed by the column reference, where the
code R indicates the row and C the column (e.g.
R12C2).

2.3.2   Entering data

In order to put data into a cell, you first have to select the cell. This is done using the cursor keys or by clicking on it with the mouse. In a worksheet, the mouse pointer is the shape of a broad cross. The marking around A1 indicates that it is active. The active cell's reference is given in the reference area.

The data for a cell are entered in the formula bar. If you make a typing mistake, erase it using the backspace key or move the cursor using the cursor keys and insert the omitted characters.

Only when you have completed the data entry by pressing Enter or clicking on the enter box (the button with the tick which appears on the left of the input line as soon as you start typing), the data entered will appear in the cell. You can interrupt data entry by pressing the Esc key or by clicking on the cancel box (the box with the cross beside the enter box).

When entering data, you must always carry out these three steps:

1   Select a cell using the mouse or the cursor keys.

2   Enter the data in the formula bar.

3   Confirm the entry for the selected cell by pressing Enter or clicking on the enter box.

2.3.3   Activating a cell or a range

Commands and functions relate to individual cells or groups of cells which must be selected before the command or function is implemented. A group of adjacent cells in rows and/or columns is known as a **range**. EXCEL marks a selected range in black. The previous illustration shows three marked ranges:

a) column C
b) row 11
c) cells E4 to F6 inclusive.

Each range has a reference, in the same way as each individual cell. This consists of the coordinates of the cell in the top left-hand corner of the range and those of the bottom right-hand cell. The coordinates of both corner cells are separated from each other by a colon, e.g. E4:F6.

It is also possible to assign a name to references and ranges. Later you will find out how you can use this to make working with formulas and functions much easier.

To select cells and ranges, you must master the following techniques:

object to be selected	operation
a cell	click on the cell
an entire column	click on the column heading
an entire row	click on the row heading
several adjacent columns	move the mouse to the left column heading and drag towards the right column heading
several adjacent rows	move the mouse to the top row heading and drag towards the bottom row heading
several cells in one row, in a column or in rows and columns	move the mouse to the top left-hand cell and drag towards the bottom right-hand cell
several isolated cells and ranges	hold down the Ctrl key and select the various cells and/or ranges in succession.

2.4   Creating a worksheet

You will now learn the basic skills required to create a worksheet, using a number of examples.

Question 2-1

The company COMPUWORLD sells non-branded computers and accessories. There are four branches. The company management wants to produce a summary of AT and 386 computers sold in January per branch and totally. Furthermore, the branches' turnover must be expressed as a percentage of total turnover.

2.4.1   Setting up the worksheet structure

It is not a good idea to start a worksheet without any prior knowledge. Particularly when compiling more complex summaries and calculations, it is recommended that you thoroughly define the problem first of all, in order to prevent errors and save time.

That is why you must answer the following questions before starting:

■ What is the purpose of the worksheet?
■ What data is available?
■ What calculations can be used to achieve the results?
■ How can the data be usefully arranged in the worksheet?

Then proceed as follows:

1 Start EXCEL or open a new worksheet.

2 Enter the constant data (headings, references, etc.).

3 Enter the variable data.

4 Enter the formulas required to calculate the results.

5 Select the required format, if the standard format is not satisfactory.

6 Determine page layout for printing, if the worksheet is to be printed out.

7 It is a good idea to save the worksheet at the end of each stage to make sure that nothing is lost.

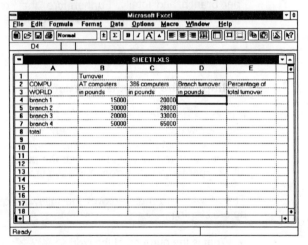

2.4.2   Entering text

The previous illustration shows the structure of the worksheet. We shall start by entering the column and row titles, which can be done in various ways.

Entering data in a cell

Click on cell B1. The frame around the cell indicates that the cell is active and that data can be entered. Type 'Turnover' in the formula bar. The text appears simultaneously in B1. Press Enter or click on the enter box to confirm.

Entering data into adjacent cells

Adjacent cells B2 to E2 are intended for the column titles. Activate these cells by moving the mouse to B2, pressing the left mouse button and dragging the mouse to E2. Cell B2 is now active and cells C2 to E2 inclusive are highlighted. Type 'AT Computers' and confirm the entry by clicking on the enter box. The next cell in the marked range, C2, is now active. Copy the entry for this cell and for D2 and E2 from the previous illustration.

Type 'COMPU' in cell A2 and 'WORLD' in cell A3.

You will have noticed that the standard column width is too narrow for some of the things we have entered. We shall therefore change the column width. Drag the mouse over column headings A to E to select these columns, then select the *Column Width* command from the *Format* menu and type '15' in the *Column Width* box. Confirm the dialog box by clicking *OK*. The cells will now be wide enough. Section 2.6.2 contains further information about adapting column widths.

Entering row titles is the same as entering column titles. Mark cells A4 to A8 inclusive. Copy the required data from the illustration. This time, confirm the entry with Enter.

Instead of using Enter, you could have moved the down cursor key to confirm the data entered. In that case, you would not have had to select the range beforehand.

Copy text

Cells B3 to D3 must contain the text 'in pounds'. You could enter this text in the way described above, but we would like to show you another way. Type the text in cell B3 alone. Then use the mouse to click on *Edit* in the menu bar and select the *Copy* command from this menu, also using the mouse. Select the paste area, i.e.

the cells to which you want to copy the contents of B3, in this case cells C3 and D3. When you have confirmed the paste area by pressing Enter, the contents of cell B3 will also appear in cells C3 and D3.

Brief summary of copying stages:

1 Select the cells or range to be copied.

2 Choose the *Copy* command from the *Edit* menu.

3 Select the paste area.

4 Confirm the copying process by pressing Enter.

Finally, in cell E3 type 'total turnover'.

If text does not fit into a cell, it will spill over into the next cell, provided the next cell is empty. If it is not, the text will be cut. However, EXCEL does store the entire text internally.

2.4.3   Entering values

Apart from the ten digits (0 to 9), numbers are made up of the characters - , +, E and e.

EXCEL accepts the following number formats:

- whole numbers   567   -567
- decimals   5.67   0.567 5,670.89 -5,670.89
- floating point
  numbers   5.89e1 5.89-E11

Other formats are interpreted as text.

Numbers entered directly into cells are known as **constants**. A point (.) is used to separate decimals. In addition to the formats mentioned above, when entering constants you can also use the following characters:

(
)
£
%

,

You should enter a minus sign before negative numbers. In addition, you can also put a negative number in
parentheses. In large numbers, a comma can be used
to separate thousands. Entering £/$ before a number,
or the % character after it, automatically changes the
standard number notation into pounds/dollars or percentages respectively.

If you exceed the cell width when entering a number
value, the error value ########## appears in the relevant cell. However, the value entered is stored correctly
internally. EXCEL operates internally with an accuracy
of 15 decimal places. The number range is from
2.225E-307 to 1.789E305.

Note:
If numbers are rounded off or not displayed entirely accurately, there may be differences between the **displayed** and the **stored** value of a cell, which can give
the impression that the formulas are producing incorrect
results. The value 5.013 is thus displayed as £5.01 in
the £ format, and the value 5.017 as £5.02. Internally,
however, EXCEL calculates using the values entered.
There will be no such problems when entering the
values in our exercise however. From the first illustration of section 2.4.4, copy the turnover data for cells B4
to C7 as whole numbers.

2.4.4   Using formulas

Before entering formulas into the exercise worksheet,
we should discuss the structure of formulas.

Compiling formulas

The operations included in a formula are geared to the problem to be solved. You **yourself** are always responsible for the **logical problem-oriented accuracy** of a formula. EXCEL also produces results if a formula is formally correct, but logically incorrect. For precisely this reason, it is absolutely essential to analyse thoroughly the problem to be solved.

In EXCEL, a **formula** is a series of values, cell references, names, functions or operations in a cell, which calculates a new value using the current values. The **current values** may be constant components of the formula or may already be in other cells on the worksheet and be addressed in the formula via the **cell references**. The calculations performed by a formula are determined by **operators** and **functions**.

EXCEL recognises four types of operators:

arithmetical operators

+	(plus sign)	addition
-	(minus sign)	subtraction
-	(minus sign)	negation
/	(slash)	division
*	(asterisk)	multiplication
%	(percentage sign)	percentages (value/100)
^	(caret)	exponentiation

text operators

| & | (ampersand) | join strings |

comparison operators

=	equal
>	greater than
<	less than
<=	less than or equal to
>=	greater than or equal to
<>	not equal to

reference operators

| : | (colon) | range |

(comma)	union
(space)	intersection

The **arithmetical operators** need no further explanation.

Using the **text operator**, you can link two or more text values to make a new text value. The **reference operators** produce the logical value TRUE or FALSE, based on the comparison of two values.

In **reference operators**, the range operator (:) separates the beginning and end of a series of adjacent cells, e.g. E10:E15. The union operator (,) is used for the notation of a series of nonadjacent cells, e.g. E10,G2,H13.

The **subset operator** addresses all cells which appear in both ranges. In the example E10:E18 E17:E25 the intersection operator produces cells E17 and E18 as an intersection. In the example E10:E18 E19:E20 the result is #NIL because there are no common cells.

Formulas are usually worked out from left to right. However, this rule is broken if several operators of differing rank appear in a formula. The following order then applies:

:	range
space	intersection
,	union
-	negation
%	percent
^	exponentiation
* or /	multiplication or division
+ or -	addition or subtraction
&	text operator
=, <, <=, >, >=, <>	comparison operators

This hierarchical order can be suppressed using parentheses. The calculations are still executed from left to right but the operations in parentheses are then performed first, with the order mentioned above applying

within the parentheses. In the following example, the
order for executing the formula is given underneath it:

```
A15*B7/((B18-420)/F2)*14
  1   4     2     3   5
```

Entering formulas
Before a formula can be entered, the required cell must
be selected using the cursor keys or the mouse. Every
formula starts with an equal sign (=), followed by formula consisting of cell references, names, text, functions or
operators.

Entering formulas takes place in the formula bar. Remember that a formula must not contain any spaces. A
formula has a maximum length of 255 characters. You
will learn various methods of specifying cell references,
names and functions in formulas.

Until the input of a formula is concluded by pressing
Enter or clicking on the enter box, you can use all the
processing possibilities available for text and values.
You can also interrupt input using Esc or by clicking on
the cancel box. By selecting the *Clear* command from
the *Edit* menu immediately after confirmation, the formula can be cancelled. Later on, the formula can also
be deleted using the *Delete* command in the *Edit* menu.

Entering formulas:

step	operation
1 activate cell for formula	cursor keys or click with mouse
2 switch on formula entry mode	=
3 type the formula in the formula bar without spaces	

4 confirm entry   Enter, cursor keys or click on
                            the enter box

Entering formulas using the keyboard

We shall demonstrate the various ways of entering a
formula using question 2-1. Firstly, in cell B8 the sum of
cells B4 to B7 must be calculated. When you have selected cell B8, type in the formula bar:

=B4+B5+B6+B7

When you have confirmed the entry by pressing Enter,
the result of the calculation is in the active cell, B8.

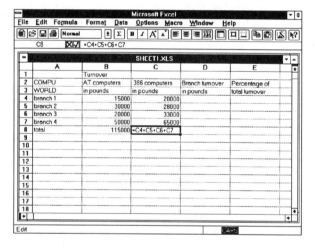

Entering formulas using the mouse

The same calculation must be performed in C8. The illustration above shows the formula in the formula bar
and in the result cell.

Rather than entering formulas using the keyboard, it is
safer to select operands using the mouse. After selecting the result cell and typing =, click the mouse on the
first cell included in the calculation, C4. The reference to
this cell is automatically included in the formula and

placed in the result cell. After entering the + you can select the next cell, C5, with the mouse. These stages, selecting the next cell with the mouse and typing +, can be
repeated until the formula is complete. The input can
also be confirmed by clicking the mouse on the enter
box.

If several successive cells have to be included in the
same formula, a particularly effective method is available for entering the formula. We can use this method in
our exercise for calculating the turnover per branch in
column D. Using the mouse, select cells D4 to D8 inclusive. After typing =, click on B4. Then type + and click
on cell C4. The formula bar now contains the formula
B4+C4. If you now confirm this using Ctrl-Enter, the formula is included in the entire marked ranged (D4:D8).
The following thus applies for entering a formula in a
range:

step	**operation**
1 select range for the formula	drag mouse over the range
2 switch on formula entry mode	=
3 type, without spaces, only the formula for the first cell in the marked range	
4 confirm entry	Ctrl-Enter

Relative and Absolute references
In the exercise, the calculation of the turnover per
branch, expressed in percentage of total turnover, is still
missing from column E. The calculation is as follows:

branch turnover * 100 / total turnover

This calculation must be entered in cells E4 to E7 inclusive. If you now try to apply the procedure just described of copying formulas in ranges, you are in for a surprise. Give it a try anyway. After confirming the formula D4*100/D8, a valid value only appears in cell E4. The other cells in the range (E5:E7) contain an error value, i.e. '#DIV/0!'. This is shown in the illustration below:

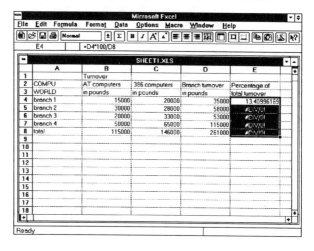

The formula was correct for the first result cell, E4, because the branch turnover in cell D4 has to be multiplied by 100 and then divided by the total turnover in cell D8. But since the references in the formula are applied **relatively** with respect to the corresponding result cell, errors automatically occur in the other cells, E5 to E7 inclusive.

The previous illustration shows the incorrect formula for cell E5 in the formula bar. The relevant branch turnover (D5) is multiplied by 100. This is correct. However, the result is not divided by total turnover (D8). In copying, EXCEL has placed cell D9 in the formula. Relatively speaking this is probably correct, but is incorrect for our calculation.

In order to calculate the share of the total percentage for each of the four branches, the product of the branch turnover*100 must be divided by the total turnover in cell D8. We must therefore give cell D8 an **absolute reference.** This is done by placing a dollar sign ($) before the column letter and row number of the cell coordinates, i.e. $D$8.

Correct the mistake now. After clicking on cell E4, the formula appears in the formula bar. Replace D8 with $D$8.

Note:
This entire replacement procedure can also be carried out using the mouse. First place the mouse pointer immediately in front or behind of the reference to be changed D8. Then select the *Reference* command from the *Formula* menu. The reference has now changed to $D$8. If you start the command again, the references changes to D$8, and the next time to $D8.

Confirm the formula and copy it to cells E5 to D8 inclusive. Your worksheet should now look like this:

	A	B	C	D	E
1		Turnover			
2	COMPU	AT computers	386 computers	Branch turnover	Percentage of
3	WORLD	in pounds	in pounds	in pounds	total turnover
4	branch 1	15000	20000	35000	13.40996169
5	branch 2	30000	28000	58000	22.22222222
6	branch 3	20000	33000	53000	20.30651341
7	branch 4	50000	65000	115000	44.06130268
8	total	115000	146000	261000	100

EXCEL therefore recognises **relative** (D8), **mixed** (D$8) and **absolute** ($D$8) references. Section 2.8.5 also gives further information about external references. You can refer to a cell or range in another worksheet using an external reference.

2.4.5 Protecting cells and formulas

Data are often entered into the wrong cells accidentally or without authorisation, which means that the data or formulas in the relevant cells are lost. It may then be impossible to reconstitute the worksheet as it previously was. You can prevent this happening by protecting your worksheet.

Using the *Cell Protection* command from the *Format* menu, you can block or hide the cells in a worksheet or macrosheet. This protection can also be linked to a **password**.

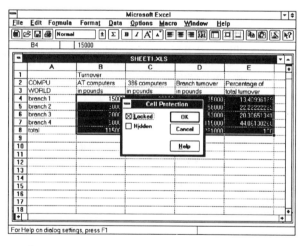

Locking prevents the contents of a cell from being changed. **Hiding** ensures that a formula is no longer given in the menu bar when the relevant cell is activated. All the cells in a new worksheet are safeguarded as standard. However, this protection only becomes operational when you choose the *Protect Document* command from the *Options* menu.

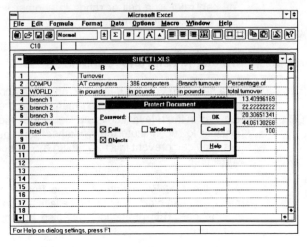

We shall now lock and hide all cells containing formulas. This involves ranges B8:C8 and D4:E8. Since all the cells in the worksheet are locked as standard, we must first suppress locking for the cells where formulas are to be entered later on (B4:C7).

step	operation
1 select range to be unlocked	drag the mouse across the range B4:C7
2 choose the *Cell Protection* command from the *Format* menu	click in the menu
3 suppress locking in the *Cell Protection* dialog box	click on the *Locked* check box

4	choose the *OK* button	click on the button
5	select the range to be hidden	press the Ctrl key and drag the mouse across ranges B8:C8 and D4:E8
6	choose the *Cell Protection* command from the *Format* menu	click in the menu
7	activate the *Hidden* option	click on the *Hidden* check box
8	choose the *OK* button	click on the button
9	choose the *Protect Document* comm and from the *Options* menu	click in the menu
10	choose *Cells* in the dialog box	click on the check box
11	choose the *OK* button in the dialog window	click on the button

If you click on a formula cell now, the formula will not be displayed. Any attempt to enter data in a formula cell will be prevented and you will see the message 'Locked cells cannot be changed'.

Now, only the required data can be entered in the work-sheet. Other procedures are not possible, except when document protection has been suppressed. You are now going to do that by clicking on *Unprotect Document* in the *Options* menu. The previous situation is now re-stored.

2.5   Worksheet management

2.5.1   Saving worksheets

We have now completed a major stage in our exercise by entering formulas. It is now a good idea to save the worksheet on harddisk or diskette. EXCEL offers three ways of doing this in the *File* menu:

- *Save*
- *Save As*
- *Save workbook.*

Save a new worksheet
When you save a new worksheet, you must give it a name. Choose the *Save as* command from the *File* menu when you save a worksheet for the first time. A dialog box appears on the screen and in the enter box EXCEL suggests a name for the worksheet, e.g. SHEET1.XLS. Change the name to EXAMP1.

The name must not contain more than eight characters. You can use upper and lower case letters. In other respects, the usual DOS conventions for file names apply. You are not obliged to give an extension. If you choose a file name with no full stop or extension, EXCEL automatically uses the following extensions:

file type	extension
worksheet	.XLS
chart	.XLC
macrosheet	.XLM
workbook	.XLW

Our exercise, to which we gave the name EXAMP1, will therefore be saved as EXAMP1.XLS. The worksheet is not closed so we can continue working. The title bar shows the worksheet's new name.

A worksheet is always saved in the current directory. We are in the C:\EXCEL directory. Since we want to store all our exercises in the C:\EXCEL\EXERCISE subdirectory, we have to double-click on its name in the *Directories* list when saving the worksheet.

Then click on *OK.* The worksheet is now saved on the harddisk and can be reloaded into the RAM at any time, even if you have quit EXCEL in the interim period.

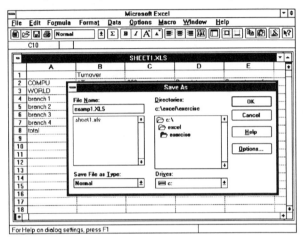

Using *Save Files as Type* in the *Save As* window, a drop-down menu will show the various file formats in which you can save a worksheet. You can choose from:

Normal   The file is saved in EXCEL format. EXCEL chooses this format automatically if you do not give an extension.

Template   The file will be saved as an EXCEL template with the extension .XLT.

Excel 3.0   The file will be saved in EXCEL 3.0 format.

Excel 2.1	The file will be saved in EXCEL 2.1 format.
SYLK	Symbolic Link - File format for data exchange with MULTIPLAN for example.
Text	Text and values will be saved as they appear in the worksheet. Columns are separated by tabs and rows by returns.
CSV	Comma Separate Values - the same as **Text** format, but a comma is used for separation.
WKS	LOTUS 1-2-3 version 1A and SYMPHONY file format.
WK1	LOTUS 1-2-3 version 2 file format.
WK3	LOTUS 1-2-3 version 3 file format.
DIF	Data Interchange Format - this file format saves only values, not formulas. File format for data exchange with VISICALC.
DBF2	dBASE II file format.
DBF3	dBASE III(+) file format.
DBF4	dBASE IV file format.

Text (Macintosh) .

Formats **CSV** and **Text** are available in DOS, MacIn-

tosh and OS/2 variations. This offers data exchange fa-
cilities with other systems.

The dialog box also gives you the opportunity of protecting your file using a sixteen-character **password** (in the
Save Options dialog box). Without the password, the
file cannot be loaded. Choose a password which you
can easily remember, but which is not easy to guess. If
you forget your password, you cannot open the worksheet.

You can also instruct EXCEL to save the old version of
the worksheet as a backup, every time you save that
worksheet after working on it (*Create Backup File* check
box). In this way, the previously saved version of the
worksheet is always available. EXCEL assigns the extension .BAK to backup copies.

Note:
It is possible to save a worksheet several times using a
different name. This is useful for comparing a particular
version of the worksheet with the current version.

Exercise 1

Save the exercise worksheet again in the EXERCISE
subdirectory, giving it the name EXAMP0. This is done
as follows:

step	operation
1 open the *File* menu	click
2 choose the *Save As* command	click
3 give the name	c:\excel\exercise\examp0
4 choose the *OK* button	click

Saving a worksheet again

To save a worksheet again, which has already been saved on the harddisk, simply choose the *Save* command from the *File* menu. The worksheet will be saved again on the harddisk. The new version replaces the old one.

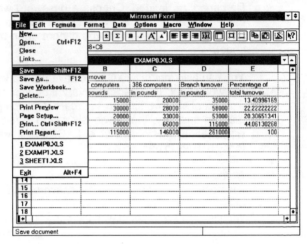

2.5.2   Deleting a saved worksheet

In the *File* menu, EXCEL also offers the possibility of deleting worksheets from the disk which are no longer required, using the *Delete* command. When you start this command, a dialog box appears. Here you will see which drive and directory are current. You will also find two menus with scroll bars which you can use to choose which file is to be deleted.

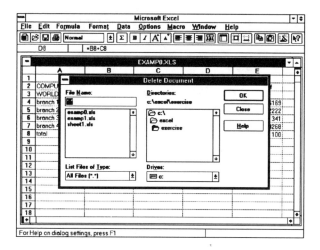

If the worksheet to be erased is not in the current directory, first choose the relevant drive and then the relevant directory. Move through the list until you find the required drive letter. Click on the drive letter to see a list of the directories in the relevant drive. Choose the directory by double-clicking.

The *File Name* list shows the files and subdirectories in the chosen drive and directory. You can move through the list using the scroll bar until you find the file to be erased. Then select it by clicking on it with the mouse. The name of the file appears in the *File Name* box.

To interrupt the erase operation, click on the *Close* button. Confirm the erase operation by clicking on the *OK* button. To make sure you want to erase, EXCEL requests further confirmation. The file is then erased.

Exercise 2

Now erase file EXAMP0.XLS from the C:\EXCEL\ EXERCISE directory.

Provided you are in the C:\EXCEL directory, you should
proceed as follows:

step		operation
1	choose the *Delete* command from the *File* menu	click
2	look for the EXER-CISE subdirectory in the *Directories* menu	click on the scroll bar
3	select the EXER-CISE directory name	double-click on EXERCISE
4	look for file name EXAMP0.XLS in the *List of Files*	click on the scroll bar
5	select file name EXAMP0.XLS	click on EXAMP0.XLS
6	message: 'Delete file 'C:\EXCEL\EXER-CISE\EXAMP0.XLS'?'	click on *YES* button

2.5.3   Loading a worksheet

Both **load** and **open** refer to the transfer of a saved
worksheet from the disk to the RAM. In terms of operation, opening is very like erasing.

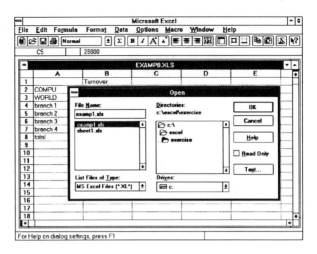

After clicking on the *Open* command in the *File* menu, the dialog window *Open* appears on the screen, giving the current drive and directory. Using the *File Name* and *Directories* menus, you can choose which worksheet to load.

You can make a preselection via the *File Name* text box, using the standard setting *.XL*. For example, by changing the standard setting to ***.XLC** you can request a list of all **chart files**. This preselection makes it much simpler to search through large directories.

A protected file can only be loaded when the correct password is given. During loading, the mouse pointer changes to an hourglass. To the left of the reference area the file format also appears (e.g. EXCEL or SYLK) and the percentage loaded at that time.

If a worksheet is already in the EXCEL application window before you open another worksheet, it stays in the RAM and on the screen. The other worksheet is overlaid on it in a new document window.

The number of worksheets which can be loaded at any one time depends on the amount of available RAM. It is possible to switch between worksheet windows using the *Window* menu. At the bottom of this menu you will see a list of all open worksheets. The worksheet in the foreground is marked with a tick. To move another worksheet into the foreground, simply click on its name. Using the *Arrange* option from the *Window* menu, EXCEL also makes it possible to display all open work-sheets alongside each other in their own window.

Note:
It is a good idea to remove from the screen and RAM all worksheets no longer required for the current operation. You can do this by bringing the worksheet to be closed into the foreground by clicking anywhere in the work space, and closing it using the *Close* command in the *File* menu. If you have changed the worksheet since it was last saved, EXCEL asks if you are sure you want to save it. It is now closed, i.e. removed from the screen and the RAM.

To close **all** loaded worksheets simultaneously, open the *File* menu by clicking on it while holding down the Shift key. This changes the *Close* command into *Close All*.

Exercise 3

We want to continue working with the worksheet we have saved as EXAMP1.XLS in the C:\EXCEL\EXER-CISE directory. Proceed as follows:

step	operation
1 choose the *Open* command from the *File* menu	double-click on it
2 search for the EXERCISE subdi-rectory in the *Direc-tories* option list	click on the scroll bar

3 select the EXER-CISE subdirectory	double-click on EXERCISE
4 search for file name EXAMP1.XLS in the *File Name* option list	click on the scroll bar
5 select file name EXAMP1.XLS	click on EXAMP1.XLS

2.6 Formatting a worksheet

This section deals with how you can change the format of a table. It is essential to remember:

- The format of a cell only influences the way it is displayed, not the value it contains.
  Only when you switch on *Precision as Displayed* in the *Sheet Options* of *Calculation* in the *Options* menu, will EXCEL calculate using the values as displayed in the worksheet.
- The format of a cell or range can be determined either before or after entering the data.
- If the cell's contents are erased, the format remains intact. This must be erased separately.
- When copying a cell or range, the format will be copied at the same time.

2.6.1 Number format

Until now we have not dealt with the format of worksheet EXAMP1.XLS. All the number values in the worksheet are still in standard format. This setting displays numbers with the greatest accuracy as whole numbers, with decimals or, if the number is too wide for the cell, in floating comma format.

In our example it would be a good idea to deviate from

the standard format for the turnover figures and percentages. We want to display the turnover figures as whole numbers with a comma separating thousands, we wish to place a £ sign in front, and percentages should be rounded up to one decimal place. We don't want the percentage sign, however.

step   **operation**

1 choose cells to be   click on the cell or drag the
   formatted   mouse over the range

2 choose the *Num-*   double-click
   ber command from
   the *Format* menu

3 choose the format   click on format bar, click on
   and adapt if   required format, adapt format
   necessary   using keyboard

4 confirm choice   click on the *OK* button

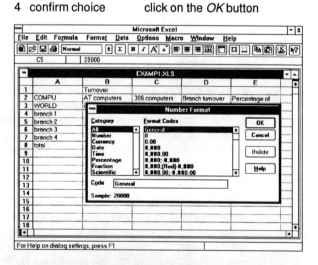

Once you have chosen the *Number* command in the *Format* menu, you will see a dialog box containing an option list of the various format possibilities for num-

bers, data and times. Click to choose the desired format, which then appears in the enter box so that you
can use it. Confirm your choice with *OK*.

EXCEL has several built-in format options for number
formatting. These are types of templates where special
format symbols are used to display numbers in the formatted cells. The following examples show how the
number 1234.567 can be displayed, in various formats,
both as a positive and as a negative.

format	positive	negative
General	1234.567	-1234.567
0	1235	-1235
0.00	1234.57	-1234.57
#,##0	1,235	-1,235
#,##0.00	1,234.57	-1,234.57
£#,##0,-£#,##	£1,235	-£1,235
£#,##0,[RED]-£#,##0	£1,235	-£1,235
£#,##0.00,-£#.##0.00	£1,234,57	-£1,234.57
£#,##0.00,[RED]-£#,##0.00	£1,234.57	-£1,234.57
0%	1234567%	-1234567%
0.00%	123456,70%	-123456,70%
0.00E+00	1.23E+03	-1.23E+03
#?/?	1234 4/7	-1234 4/7
#??/??	1234 55/97	-1234 55/97

The format symbols you can also use to define a number format yourself have the following meanings:

symbol	meaning
General	display in standard format.
0	digit placeholder.

If the format contains more zeroes than
the digits in the number to be formatted,
zeroes are added left of the point. Empty
spaces to the right of the point are also
filled in with zeroes. If the number of digits
behind the point is greater than the number of placeholders behind the point, the

number is rounded up. All digits in front of
the point are always shown, even if placeholders are missing.

Thus, using the format 000.00 the number
4123.5 is shown as 4123.50, and the number 12,568 becomes 012.57, using the
same format.

\#   digit placeholder.
             Unlike the zero placeholder, only the digits
             actually present in the number to be for-
             matted are shown.
             Using the format #0.## the number 5.1 re-
             mains 5.1.

?   placeholder for a digit.
             The same applies as for the zero digit
             placeholder, except that unimportant ze-
             roes on the left or right of the decimal point
             are replaced by a space.

.   decimal point.
             There must always be a zero as the first
             location identifier in front of the point.

,   separator for thousands.

%   percentage sign.
             The number given is divided by 100 and
             shown with a percentage sign after it.

E-E+e-e+   floating comma notation.

:-+£   the corresponding sign is shown with the
             format. All other signs must be placed in
             inverted commas ("").
             e.g.: £#,##0.00 "debit"

*   the sign following the asterisk is repeated
             until the cell is full.
             e.g.:*-#0.0 |----------12.31

@   placeholder for text.

[RED]   the value in the cell is shown in the colour
                given in the square brackets. Obviously,
                this only applies if you have a colour
                screen. The following colours are
                possible: BLACK, BLUE, CYAN, GREEN,
                PURPLE, RED, WHITE and YELLOW.

The number format consists of a maximum of three
number sections. If you wish, you can insert text after
them. The individual sections of a number format are
separated from each other by a semi-colon. The number sections contain the following notations.

If there are three number sections:

a) the first section contains the notation for positive
   numbers
b) the second section contains the notation for negative
   numbers
c) the third section contains the notation for zeroes.
   e.g.: [BLUE]#,##0.00"D",[RED]-#,##0.00"C",0

If there are two number sections:

a) the first section contains the notation for positive
   numbers
b) the second section contains the notation for negative
   numbers.
   e.g.: £#,##0.00,-£#,##0.00

If there is one number section only, the notation applies to all numbers.
   e.g.: *=£#,##0.00" VAT"

Exercise 4

You now have sufficient knowledge to format the numbers in worksheet EXAMP1.XLS.

1 Format for turnover figures:
   Use the mouse to select range B4:D8.
   Choose the *Number* command from the *Format*
   menu.
   From the option list (*All*), choose format £#,##0.00,"-
   "£#,##0.00.
   Confirm your choice with *OK*.

2 Format for percentages:
   Use the mouse to select the range E4:E8.
   Choose the *Number* command from the *Format*
   menu.
   From the option list (*All*), choose format #,##0.00. In
   the *Code* text box, erase the second zero behind the
   point.
   Confirm your choice with *OK*.

Do not forget to save the worksheet now and again.
Save it using the *Save As* command from the *File* menu
and using file name EXAMP1A.XLS.

			Microsoft Excel	

File Edit Formula Format Data Options Macro Window Help

	A	B	C	D	E
1		Turnover			
2	COMPU	AT computers	386 computers	Branch turnover	Percentage of
3	WORLD	in pounds	in pounds	in pounds	total turnover
4	branch 1	£15,000.00	£20,000.00	£35,000.00	13.4
5	branch 2	£30,000.00	£28,000.00	£58,000.00	22.2
6	branch 3	£20,000.00	£33,000.00	£53,000.00	20.3
7	branch 4	£50,000.00	£65,000.00	£115,000.00	44.1
8	total	£115,000.00	£146,000.00	£261,000.00	100.0
9					
10					
11					
12					
13					
14					
15					
16					
17					
18					

Ready

Note:
The format you have changed is included in the option
list as a new format variable. It is therefore possible to
define a format yourself, in which case you should ad-

here to the rules described above. It is also possible to erase formats you no longer require from the list. This is done by selecting the relevant format from the option list and then clicking on the *Delete* button.

2.6.2 Defining column widths and row heights

The standard column width is set at ten characters. In reality, the number of characters which will fit into a cell depends on the font, letter size and any styles such as bold and italic.

In order to change the column width, you only need to select one cell from the relevant column. If you want to change the width of several columns, simply select a row of cells. Then choose the *Column Width* command from the *Format* menu. Now enter the desired width in the *Column Width* box. You can return to the standard width by checking on the *Use Standard Width* box.

You will see that the *Column Width* dialog box also contains the button *Best Fit.* You can use this button to adapt the column width to the contents of the cell.

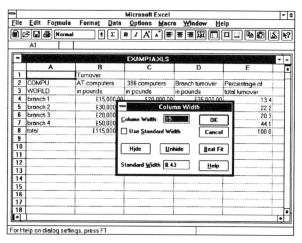

There is also a simpler way of changing the column width. Place the mouse pointer on the gridline to the right of the title of the column whose width you want to change.

As you see, the shape of the mouse pointer changes into a vertical line with arrows pointing to the left and to the right. If you drag the mouse pointer to the right, you will continuously widen the column. A column cannot be made wider than the window.

By dragging the mouse to the left, you can make the column narrower until it has disappeared altogether. The column is then hidden, but that does not mean that the values in it have disappeared. If you wish, you can make the column visible again. In the *Column Width* dialog box you will see *Hide* and *Unhide* buttons. Use these to perform the same functions.

Exercise 5

1 Change the column width in worksheet EXAMP1A.XLS as follows:
   Column A 12
   Columns B, C and D 13
   Column E 17

2 In cell C1, type 'January'.

3 Save the worksheet.

Unlike the column width, the row height is automatically adapted to the font you choose. It is also possible to change the row height using a dialog box or directly using the mouse. However, the row height is only adapted automatically if the standard height applies to a row.

To change the row height, first select the relevant row in a cell. If you want to change the height of all the rows in the worksheet, click on a column heading. Then, from the *Format* menu, choose the *Row Height* command. When you have filled in the desired height, confirm this by clicking on the *OK* button.

The row height can also be changed using the mouse. Place the mouse pointer in the row title for the relevant row on the horizontal gridline. The mouse pointer changes into a horizontal line with arrows pointing up and down. To increase the row height, drag the mouse downwards. If you drag the mouse upwards, the row height will decrease.

Exercise 6

1 Change the row height of rows 2 and 3 of worksheet EXAMP1A.XLS to 19.5.

2 Save the worksheet.

3 Compare the result with the illustration below:

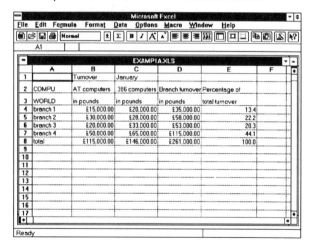

2.6.3   Choosing fonts

Depending on the type of printer connected, EXCEL offers a wide range of fonts in varying sizes and styles.
You can choose a combination of font, size and style for
a particular cell, for a range or for an entire worksheet.

This is how you change the font. First, select the cell or
range where you want to change the font and then
choose the *Font* command from the *Format menu.* The
dialog box which appears on your screen contains font
and font size option lists. By clicking, select the desired
options. In the *Sample* box, you will see a preview of the
chosen settings. If you wish, you can also specify a colour using the *Color* option list. The altered text format
only applies to the selected cell or range. The other
cells in the worksheet retain the standard text format.

We are now going to change the text format of cells A2
and A3 of worksheet EXAMP1A.XLS, which is still on
the screen. Select the *Font* command from the *Format*
menu. Do not change the MS Sans Serif font in the *Font*
option list. Change the size to 14. Using the scroll bar,
move through the list and select the desired size by
clicking on it. Choose bold as the *Style.* Confirm the
changed format by clicking on *OK.*

Since version 3.0, EXCEL uses so-called **styles**. A
style is a combination of format settings saved under
one name. You can use this to format a cell or a range
without having to set the individual components such as
font, size or style. When you choose a style for a cell or
range and then change this profile, the format of the cell
or range changes in accordance with the new format
settings.

All the cells in a new worksheet are automatically assigned the *Normal* style. In terms of text format, this
means MS Sans Serif, with no extra styles such as bold
or italic.

To change an existing format profile or define a new style, choose the *Style* command from the *Format* menu. You will then see this dialog box on your screen:

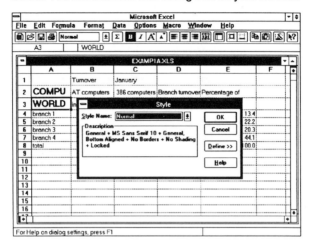

By then clicking on Define, you can now define not only the text format, but also the number format and cell format. We will come back to changing the cell format later on. Defining a new style begins by giving it a name in the *Style Name* box. If you want to change an existing style, choose the relevant profile from the option list. Below the name of the style, you will see a description and, in the *Style Includes* box you will see the elements for which a setting has been chosen. These elements correspond to the buttons below them. You use these to define the relevant element.

For example, to change the font, click on the *Font...* button in the Change box. You will recognise the dialog box which now appears on your screen from *Format - Font.* Similarly, by clicking on the Number box, call up the *Number Format* dialog box. However, the settings you can now choose do not apply to a specific cell or range, but only to the style.

Now we shall define a new style with the name 'Column

Title'. Choose the *Style* command from the *Format* menu and type this name in the *Style Name* box. Go to Define, click on it and then click on the *Font* button. The corresponding dialog box appears on your screen. Choose size 8 and bold. To include the new profile in the list, click on the *Add* button in the Style box and exit the dialog box with *OK*.

In the toolbar you will see a drop-down option list (an arrow pointing downwards) with predefined styles. This is used to assign a style to a cell or range. Select range B2:E3 by dragging the mouse over it and pull down the list of format definitions by clicking on the button, and choose *Column Title*. This style now applies to the se- lected range. As you can see, the standard text format has changed to MS Sans Serif 8 bold, the setting of the *Column Title* style.

Exercise 7

1 Choose the following format for cells B1 and C1: MS Sans Serif 12 bold italic. To do this, use the *Font* command from the *Format* menu.

2 Define the following style: Row Title: MS Sans Serif 8 bold.

3 Assign this style to the range A4:A8.

4 Compare your worksheet with the illustration below and save it using *File - Save As* under the name EXAMP2.XLS.

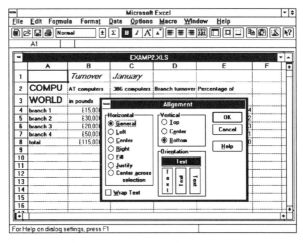

2.6.4 Aligning text and numbers

Another useful format tool is the alignment of text or numbers within a cell. Normally, EXCEL aligns text on the left and numbers on the right. Logical values and error values are centered. Using the *Alignment* command from the *Format* menu, you yourself can define how the contents of a cell or range are aligned. The command calls up the dialog box shown below:

As you can see, you can choose from *General* (the setting described above), *Left, Center, Right, Fill, Justify
and Center Across Selection*. Perhaps *Fill* requires
some explanation. When you choose *Fill,* the contents
of the selected cell are repeated until the entire cell is
filled. The dialog box also contains the check box *Wrap
Text*. If you select this option, text which does not fit in
the cell is wrapped to the next line. The row height is
automatically adapted. Briefly, the method is as follows:

1   Select the cells or ranges to be aligned.

2   Choose the *Alignment* command from the *Format*
    menu.

3   Choose the required alignment.

4   Confirm the dialog box with *OK.*

You can also set the *Left, Center* and *Right* alignment
directly using the following buttons in the toolbar:

This is done by choosing the cells to be aligned and
then clicking on one of the buttons.

The options in the *Vertical* and *Orientation* boxes are
self-explanatory.

Note:
It is also possible to include alignment in a style.

Exercise 8

1   Choose the following alignment for worksheet
    EXAMP2.XLS:
         A2:A8   right
         B2:E3   centered

2 Save the worksheet using *File - Save*.

2.6.5 Border and patterns

Unlike many other spreadsheet programs, in EXCEL you can add a border or patterns to a cell or range without having to add them to adjacent rows and columns. Briefly, this is how it's done:

1 Choose the cell or range which are to have a border.

2 Choose the *Border* command from the *Format* menu.

3 Choose the desired border, style and colour.

4 Confirm with *OK*.

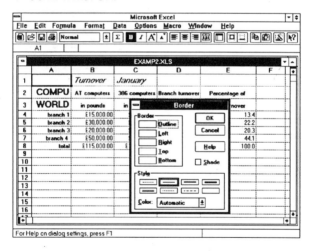

Choose the pattern in the same way, using *Format - Patterns*

You can put a border around one or more sides of the cell or range, or around its entire outline. Several border styles are available. However, it is not possible to use

more than one border style in any one cell. If you select
Shade, the cell or range will have a shaded pattern. You
can choose a colour for the border, using *Color.*

In *Format - Patterns* you can choose from a number of
patterns, for which you can also choose a foreground
and a background colour. The Sample box shows what
the chosen combination of pattern, foreground and
background colour looks like.

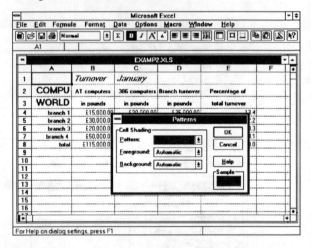

Note:
It is also possible to include the border and patterns in a
style.

Exercise 9

1   A border is to be put around ranges B1:E1, B2:B3,
    C2:C3, D2:D3, E2:E3, A4:A7 B4:B7, C4:C7, D4:D7
    and E4:E7, and cells A8, B8, C8 and D8 of work-
    sheet EXAMP2.XLS. Range A1:A3 is also to be
    shaded.
    Select the first of the above ranges. Choose the *Out-
    line* option from the *Format - Border* dialog box and
    click on *OK.*

Select the other ranges one after the other and choose the *Repeat Border* command from the *Edit* menu.
For the last range, select both *Outline* and *Shade*.

2 Save the worksheet using *File - Save*.

2.6.6 Repeating and undoing Format menu commands

All commands in the *Format* menu can be repeated or undone immediately after using them. For example, immediately after you have chosen a font, the commands *Undo Font* and *Repeat Font* are available in the *Edit* menu.
Using the first of these, you can restore the previous text format of the corresponding cell. The second is used to repeat your chosen text format for another cell or range.

It is also possible to copy a format. This is done by selecting the cell or range whose format you want to copy. Then choose the *Copy* command from the *Edit* menu and select the cell or range to which you want to copy the format. Then choose the *Paste Special* command from the *Edit* menu. The following dialog box then appears on your screen:

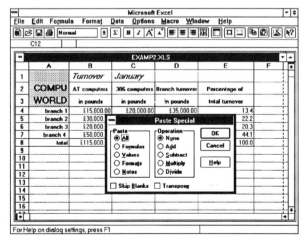

From this box choose the *Formats* command and then
click on the OK button.

2.6.7   Screen display

It is possible to turn off the gridline display option. This
is done using the *Options - Display* dialog box, and turn-
ing off *Gridlines.*

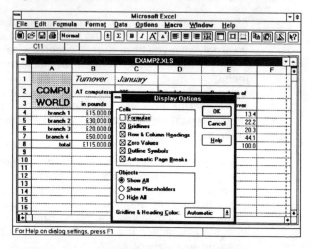

You can also turn off the row and column headings display options using this dialog box. The *Zero Values* option turns off the display of zeroes in cells with zero
values. If you select *Formulas,* instead of the results
you will see the formulas themselves. If you have a colour screen, you can specify *Gridline and Heading Color.*
You can choose from sixteen different colours.

Exercise 10

1 Turn off the gridline display option for worksheet
EXAMP2.XLS.

2 Save the worksheet using *File - Save.*

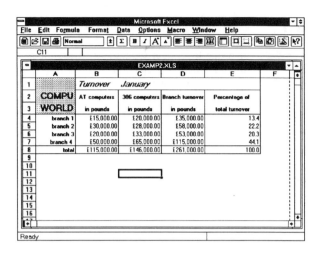

2.6.8 Drawing in a worksheet

EXCEL version 3.0 and later enables graphic objects such as lines, curves, squares, rectangles, circles and ovals to be included in a worksheet. Select the *Toolbars...* option from the *Options* menu. Then select the *Drawing* toolbar and click on *Show*. You will be presented with a workset enabling you to create all sorts of forms and shapes for use in a worksheet.

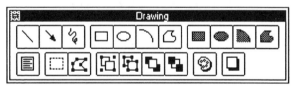

When you have drawn an object, you can edit it using the commands in the *Format* menu, after you have selected it.

2.7   Printing worksheets

In order to print a worksheet, a printer must be connected. However, this on its own is not enough. Before
you print a worksheet, you should determine the page
setup, i.e. the paper size, margins, print direction, display of row and column headings, etc.. You can only
print the worksheet after you have determined the page
setup.

2.7.1   Setting up the printer

When you installed WINDOWS, you probably installed
a printer too - in other words, copied the required printer
driver. However, it is also possible to install printers
later using the WINDOWS Control Panel. This can be
found in Main, the Program Manager.

You set the paper size, print direction, etc. using *File -
Page Setup*.

2.7.2   Making print titles

When working with large worksheets consisting of several pages, it is a good idea to print the row and column
titles on every page, which gives a better overview of
the worksheet.

You can only designate an entire row or column as a
print title. Several rows or columns can only be chosen
if they are adjacent. The rows and/or columns with print
titles must be selected. To make several selections,
hold down the Ctrl key while clicking with the mouse on
the desired row or column.

Using the *Set Print Titles* command from the *Options*
menu, you can establish the selected range as the print
title. The range is assigned the name 'Print_Titles'. You
can check this using the *Define Name* command from
the *Formula* menu. If required, you can also cancel the

print title using this dialog box.

Our worksheet does not require print titles.

2.7.3   Setting a print area

In theory, EXCEL will print all the cells in a worksheet
which contain data. However, if you only want to print a
certain section of a worksheet, you can designate this
the **print area.** This is done by selecting the desired
range and then choosing *Set Print Area* from the *Options* menu.

It is also possible to designate several ranges as print
ranges. These are then printed in the order in which you
selected them. The selected range is assigned the
name 'Print_Area'. If you want to change this name or
cancel the print range, you can do this in the *Formula -
Define Name* dialog box.

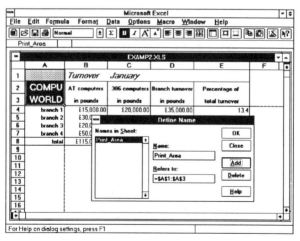

Do not include print titles in the print range since these
will then be printed twice on the first page. The print
range is indicated on the screen by a dotted line.

2.7.4   Specifying page breaks

EXCEL divides a large worksheet into pages, based on
the margins and sheet size which you specify in the *File
- Page Setup* dialog box. The program first completes
the rows and then the columns. However, you can
specify page breaks yourself using *Set Page Break*
from the *Options* menu. First, choose where you want to
start a new page. This is the cell beneath or to the right
of the page break dividing line. There are three possibilities:

■ You select a cell in column A, but not A1. The page
   break dividing line is then inserted horizontally,
   above the cell.
■ You select a cell in row 1, but not in column A. The
   page break dividing line is inserted vertically, to the
   left of the cell.
■ You select a cell which is not in column A nor row 1.
   The page break dividing line is then inserted both
   horizontally, above the cell, and vertically, to the left
   of the cell.

To remove a page break, click on one of these cells.
The *Set Page Break* command from the *Options* menu
then changes to *Remove Page Break*.

2.7.5   Specifying page setup

The *File - Page Setup* dialog box provides a number of
possibilities for changing the layout of the printer output:

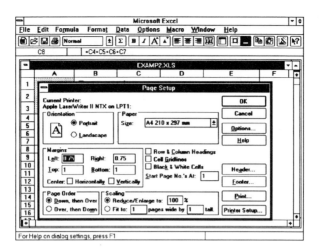

By activating the *Row and Column Headings* and *Cell Gridlines* boxes, you indicate that these are to be printed. By specifying the margins values, you set the distance between the page edges and the printed worksheet. However, these settings do not affect the position of the headers and footers, which are always approximately one inch from the lower or upper page edge and approximately 3/4 of an inch from the left-hand page edge. Choose the margins so that the worksheet is not printed on top of the headers and footers.

It is possible to specify other text as a header or footer. Choose these options (*Header* or *Footer*), if required, in the Page Setup dialog box. Headers and footers can be arranged to conform to your needs. The dialog boxes are self-explanatory. Below is a brief summary of the codes used for the layout of headers and footers:

code	effect
&L	left-aligns subsequent text
&C	centers subsequent text
&R	right-aligns subsequent text
&D	prints out current date
&T	prints out current time

&F	prints out file name
&B	makes subsequent text bold
&I	makes subsequent text italic
&&	prints a &
&P	prints the page number
&N	Prints the total number of pages

The following example is intended to clarify how to use these codes, if you do not want to use the buttons. To print out the words 'Turnover Data' on the left, italic, with the date in the middle and the name of the worksheet on the right, the following coding is used (in the 'Center Section'):

&L&ITurnover Data&C&D&R&F

Exercise 11

Choose the following settings for EXAMP2.XLS:

1 Header: on the left, the file name in bold, the text 'Exercise' centered in italics, the date on the right. (Answer: &L&B&F&C&IExercise&R&D.)

2 Footer: the text 'Page' centered, together with the page number. (Answer: &CPage &P.)

3 Margins: left 1, right 1, top 1.5, bottom 2.

4 Turn off printing of row and column headings, as well as gridlines.

Save the worksheet using *File - Save.*

2.7.6   Print Preview

Using the EXCEL preview function, you can check the settings you have chosen on screen. The worksheet is displayed exactly as it will appear on paper. This saves both time and paper if you notice things you would like to change or correct. This makes test printing virtually superfluous.

Choose the *Print Preview* command from the *File* menu to see what the worksheet will look like on paper. A new window appears on the screen containing a reduced version of the printed page.

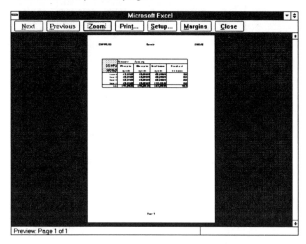

The mouse pointer now looks like a magnifying glass. If you click somewhere on the worksheet, the corresponding section will be enlarged. The operation of the buttons at the top of the window is self-explanatory.

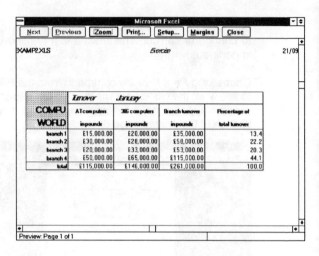

Depending on the printer, and the corresponding variations in character set and format possibilities, the result may look somewhat different on your screen.

Exercise 12

Check the format of worksheet EXAMP2.XLS and correct if necessary.

2.7.7   Printing

To print the worksheet, choose the *Print* command from the *File* menu. Via the dialog box which now appears on your screen, you can specify the number of copies you want and whether you want to print all or only specified pages. Some printers also allow you to turn off the quality function. The worksheet is then printed more quickly, but is not such good quality. Finally, in addition to the table, you can also print out the notes.

Exercise 13

Print out worksheet EXAMP2.XLS and compare the result with the illustration below:

EXAMP2.XLS   Exercise   21/09/92

	Turnover	January		
COMPU	AT computers	386 computers	Branch turnover	Percentage of
WORLD	in pounds	in pounds	in pounds	total turnover
branch 1	£15,000.00	£20,000.00	£35,000.00	13.4
branch 2	£30,000.00	£28,000.00	£58,000.00	22.2
branch 3	£20,000.00	£33,000.00	£53,000.00	20.3
branch 4	£50,000.00	£65,000.00	£115,000.00	44.1
total	£115,000.00	£146,000.00	£261,000.00	100.0

Page 1

2.8   Editing worksheets

Even when a worksheet is finished, you may want to improve its format or operation. Sometimes a worksheet has to be adapted to changed circumstances.

2.8.1   Inserting and deleting rows and columns

Let's take worksheet EXAMP2.XLS as an example. From the visual point of view, it would be better to move the table from the upper left-hand corner to the middle of the window.

Luckily, you do not need to re-create the worksheet to do this! We can solve the problem by adding some rows above the worksheet and one or more columns to the left of the worksheet.

To insert a row above row one, select the first row by clicking on the row heading. After *Edit - Insert,* a new row has been added above the one you selected. The row which was originally row 1 has now become row 2. If you want to insert more rows, just use *Repeat Insert* from the *Edit* menu. The same also applies to inserting columns.

You can also insert individual cells, rather than entire rows and columns. If you select a cell, followed by *Edit - Insert,* a dialog box appears on the screen, where you can choose *Shift Cells Right* or *Shift Cells Down.* The first of these commands inserts a new cell and shifts the selected cell to the right. The second command shifts the selected cell downwards.

To remove rows, columns or individual cells, simply follow the instructions above, but choose the *Delete* command from the *Edit* menu. If you only want to erase the **contents** of a cell, use *Edit - Clear.*

Note:
Be aware of the difference between the *Delete* and

Clear commands in the *Edit* menu. The *Clear* command only relates to the contents (All, Format, Formulas, Notes) of the selected cells. The *Delete* command removes the selected cell from the worksheet. This also affects the other cells in the worksheet since their position changes, leading to incorrect references, or references to removed cells, occurring in formulas.

Exercise 14

Insert two empty rows to worksheet EXAMP2.XLS, above the table, and one column to the left of it. Then save the worksheet using *File - Save*.

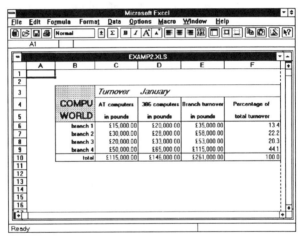

2.8.2   Moving cells and ranges

Rather than inserting rows and columns, it is also possible to move the entire table on the worksheet. EXCEL is able to move a cell range consisting of one or more cells from its current position to another, random place on the worksheet. In this event, the data, format, formulas, notes and references are also automatically moved too. This is done in two stages:

1   First select the range to be moved, in this case the whole table, and then copy it to the Clipboard, using the *Cut* command from the *Edit* menu. The table is probably still in its former position on the screen, but it now has a frame around it.

2   Now select the paste area, i.e. the place the range is to be moved to. EXCEL takes the cell you choose as the top left-hand corner of the paste area. Confirm the moving process using *Edit - Paste.* The contents of the Clipboard appears in the paste area and the table disappears from its former location. Cell references are adapted to the new situation.

You can use Esc to interrupt the move operation, and the *Undo Paste* command from the *Edit* menu to put the range back in its original position.

Exercise 15

1   Move the entire table in worksheet EXAMP2.XLS to the area beginning with C9.

2   Undo the move operation using the relevant command from the *Edit* menu.

2.8.3   Copying cells and ranges

In contrast to moving, copying does not erase the selected range from its original position. After copying, the copied cells are therefore duplicated.

EXCEL automatically adapts relative and mixed references, but absolute references remain unchanged. As with moving, when copying you select the cells you wish to copy first, and then the paste area. EXCEL offers several ways of copying. The relevant commands can be found in the *Edit* menu.

a) Copying cells to another location in the worksheet

1 Select the range to be copied.

2 Choose the *Copy* command from the *Edit* menu. A frame appears around the range to be copied.

3 Select the paste area. The cell you choose becomes the top left-hand corner of the paste area.

4 Use the *Paste* command from the *Edit* menu to copy. EXCEL now copies the selected cells, including their format, to the paste area.

b) Copying cells to several locations in a worksheet

To copy a cell or range to several locations in a worksheet, first carry out the first two steps described in a). Then select the first paste area. Select the subsequent paste areas also holding down the Ctrl key. Then choose the *Paste* command from the *Edit* menu.

c) Cell attributes

Cell attributes refer to values, formulas, format and notes. In theory, when cells are copied, all these attributes are copied with them. If, however, you choose the *Paste Special* command from the *Edit* menu, a dialog box appears on the screen, which enables you to define which of the attributes are to be copied with the cell. Furthermore, you can perform the following calculations between the cells of the copy and the paste areas:

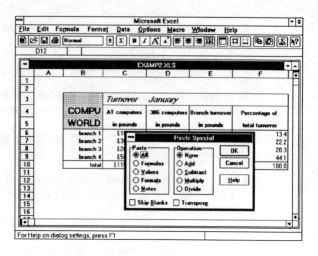

None	corresponds to *Edit - Paste*
Add	adds the contents of the copy area to that of the paste area
Subtract	subtracts the contents of the copy area from that of the paste area
Multiply	multiplies the contents of the copy area by that of the paste area
Divide	divides the contents of the paste area by that of the copy area

d) Copying to adjacent cells

Often, you may have to copy certain values or formulas from one cell to a number of adjacent cells. Due to the likelihood of making mistakes, especially in formulas, it is much safer to copy them than to enter them again via the keyboard.

For example, supposing cell A5 contains a formula which we also need in adjacent cells B5, C5 and D5.

- Select the entire range A5:D5. The cell to be copied must be the first one (i.e. on the far left) of the selected range.
- Then choose the *Fill Right* command from the *Edit* menu. The formula is now copied to the right, to cells B5, C5 and D5, and relative references are adapted. Absolute references remain unchanged.

To give another example, the text 'branch 1' must be copied from cell B6 to range B7:B13.

- Select the range B6:B13. The cell to be copied must be the first (i.e. the uppermost) of the selected range.
- Then choose the *Fill Down* command from the *Edit* menu. The text is now copied downwards to cells B7 to B13 inclusive.

If you open the Edit menu while holding down the Shift key, both copy commands change into *Fill Left* and *Fill Up.* You can now copy a cell in the right-hand column to the left, or a cell in the bottom row upwards.

Exercise 16

Widen the table in worksheet EXAMP2.XLS so that the turnover for printers can be included in it. This is done by adding a column before the 'Branch turnover' column and filling it in. Remember that the formula for calculating the branches' turnover must be adapted!

Remove the first two rows and column A. Allocate column width 13 to column F.

Compare your worksheet with the one in the illustration below and save it as EXAMP3.XLS using *File - Save As.*

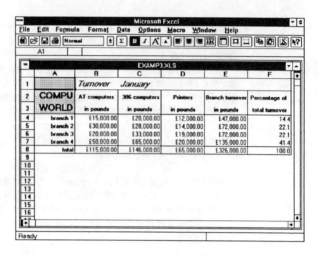

2.8.4   Splitting a worksheet window into panes

It is often useful to split up a worksheet window into panes, for example to look at different parts of the worksheet at the same time. When working with large worksheets, it is extremely handy to be able to put row and column headings in panes. You will then be able to find your way around the worksheet much more easily.

EXCEL can support a maximum of four panes per worksheet window. A worksheet window is split into two horizontally or vertically adjacent panes using the horizontal and vertical split boxes. This is done by clicking on one of the two split boxes and dragging the split bar down or to the right.

To split a window into four in one operation, choose the *Split* command from the *Window* menu of the corresponding worksheet window. A horizontal and a vertical bar appear in the worksheet. If you place the cursor on one of these bars, a double arrow will appear. You can then drag the bar to the desired point of division.

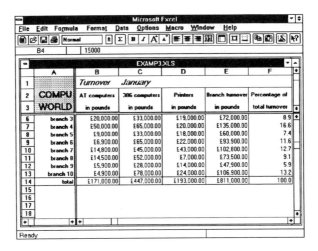

The illustration shows that the company COMPU-WORLD has opened six new branches. If we scroll through the table using the scroll bar, the column titles soon disappear. It is therefore difficult to know where you are in the worksheet. This is why we have used the Split command from the Window menu as an aid in defining the dividing line between columns A and B and rows 3 and 4. The worksheet is thus split into four panes. This can be seen from the double lines and the extra scroll bars. It is now possible to scroll through the table without the column titles disappearing from the screen.

So as not to have to split the worksheet window every time you load the window, you can use the *Freeze Panes* command from the *Window* menu. In this menu, the command then changes to *Unfreeze Panes*, so that you can cancel the split later on.

Exercise 17

Make this split in worksheet EXAMP3.XLS.

2.8.5   Linking worksheets

In addition to splitting into panes, as described above, it
is also possible to link two or more worksheets together
using formulas, so that data can be exchanged.

You will see, in the last section of this chapter, that it is
even possible to link EXCEL files with files in other programs.

Linking simplifies:

- merging data from several worksheets into one new
  worksheet
- creating worksheets with differing formats for the
  same figures
- rationalising complex models by splitting into summaries.

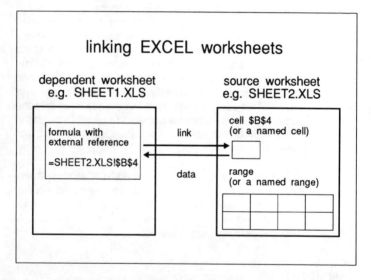

As shown in the illustration, using a formula with an external reference in a dependent worksheet, it is possible
directly to address a cell or a range in the source worksheet.

This type of formula always begins with the name of the source worksheet, followed by an exclamation mark (!) and the cell or range to which reference must be made.

e.g.:

=TURNOVER!$B$4
=C5+TURNOVER!$B$4
=F12*C5+TURNOVER!$B$4+C6*TURNOVER!$B$8

Method for linking worksheets:

1 Load the worksheets to be linked.

2 Activate the window for the source worksheet.

3 Select the cell or range to which you want to refer in the dependent worksheet.

4 Choose the *Copy* command from the *Edit* menu (a frame appears around the chosen cell).

5 Activate the window for the dependent worksheet.

6 Select the relevant cell or the upper left-hand corner of the relevant range to include the external references.

7 Choose the *Paste Link* command from the *File* menu.

Obviously, it is also possible to enter a formula with external references in the formula bar using the keyboard.

When saving, the source worksheets must always be closed before the dependent worksheet. Using the following command, we shall explain worksheet linking.

Question 2-2

The company COMPUWORLD has divided its sales market into regions - North, West and South.

A quarterly turnover summary is drawn up for each region, which includes the turnover figures for the months in the quarter per square metre of sales area, per employee and as totals. Furthermore, the table contains information about the total sales surface area and the number of employees. The illustration below shows the worksheet for the North region. The company management now wants a summary of the total quarterly turnover for the three regions per square metre and per employee, without having to re-enter the relevant data.

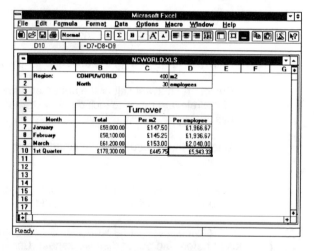

We will assume that the three worksheets for the regions have already been created and saved on the harddisk in the directory C:\EXCEL\EXERCISE under the names NCWORLD.XLS, WCWORLD.XLS and SCWORLD.XLS.

Note:

To follow the exercise more closely, it is a good idea to use worksheet NCWORLD.XLS from the previous example. You can calculate the average turnover per square metre by dividing the relevant turnover figure by the contents of cell $C$1, and the average turnover per employee by dividing the relevant turnover figure by the contents of cell $C$2.

Save the worksheet three times using *File - Save As* and use the file names given above. To obtain various values, for example, transfer the turnover figures per worksheet from the illustration below. Region West has 300 square metres and 20 employees, and region South has 300 square metres and 25 employees.

We must now create a new worksheet in which the data from the other three will be brought together. We will call this worksheet TOTWORLD.XLS. The illustration below shows what this worksheet looks like:

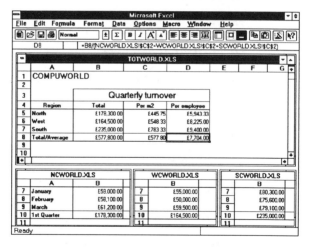

The TOTWORLD.XLS worksheet is a dependent worksheet, the other three are source worksheets. Cells B5, B6 and B7 are intended for the regional turnover figures. These will be imported as an external reference to the source worksheets. Cell B5 is to contain the total turnover for the North region. The formula for this is as follows:

=NCWORLD.XLS!$B$10

The formula for the two other regions:

=WCWORLD.XLS!$B$10
=SCWORLD.XLS!$B$10

Column C is reserved for the average turnover per square metre. The formulas for this are:

=B5/NCWORLD.XLS!$C$1
=B6/WCWORLD.XLS!$C$1
=B7/SCWORLD.XLS!$C$1

The average turnover per employee will be shown in column D. The formulas are as follows:

=B5/NCWORLD.XLS!$C$2
=B6/WCWORLD.XLS!$C$2
=B7/SCWORLD.XLS!$C$2

The absolute references in the formulas relate to the cells in the source worksheets.

Now, only the total and the averages in row 10 are missing:

■ Total turnover for all regions:

=B5+B6+B7

■ Average turnover per square metre:

=B8/(NCWORLD.XLS!$C$1+WCWORLD.XLS!$C$1+
SCWORLD.XLS!$C$1)

■ Average turnover per employee:

=B8/(NCWORLD.XLS!$C$2+WCWORLD.XLS.$C$2+ SCWORLD.XLS!$C$2)

The worksheet is complete. Save it using *File - Save As.*

We can now shrink the worksheet, as shown in the previous illustration, to open the three source worksheets and spread them across the screen in reduced form.

Each worksheet has its own window, which you activate by clicking inside it. You can tell which is the active window by its dark title bar and scroll bars.

As you can see, the values from the three regional worksheets have been transferred to the dependent worksheet TOTWORLD.XLS. If you change a value in one of the three source worksheets, this change is passed on to the TOTWORLD.XLS worksheet.

You should now be able to close all the windows individually using the *Close* command from the *File* menu, but it is also possible to close all windows simultaneously. You can do this by clicking on *File* and holding down the Shift key. The *Close* command has now changed into *Close All*, and you can use this to close all the open windows. If worksheets have been changed but not yet saved, EXCEL asks if you want to save them first.

The *File - Save Workbook* command is even more useful. EXCEL then saves a list of names of all open files and windows, together with their location on the screen. The file where this list is saved is given the name BOOK.XLW as standard. You can change this name if you wish, for example into COMPU.XLW. Furthermore, all files are saved which have been changed since the last save operation.

At a later date, if you want to arrange the files on the screen in exactly the same way, simply load the COMPU.XLW file.

2.9 Worksheets with complex formulas

2.9.1 Using names in formulas

In long formulas with a lot of cell references, it can be difficult to see what these formulas calculate and which values they use. EXCEL offers the possibility of giving names to cells, ranges, constants and even formulas, and using these names in formulas instead of cell references. This makes working with them much simpler and means that formulas are easier to understand at a glance.

Rules for using names

The following rules apply to using names:

■ All the letters and figures, together with the full stop (.) and underlining (_) can be used. The first character in a name must be a letter. Names which correspond to references are not permitted (e.g. B$3 or R1C45).

■ Spaces and hyphens may not be used, even as separators. Use underlining or a full stop instead (e.g. total_turnover).

■ A name must not contain more than 255 characters.

■ Upper and lower case letters can be mixed together.

The commands for names and using names can be found in the *Formula* menu.

Assigning a name to a cell or range

To assign a name to a cell or range, choose the *Define Name* command from the *Formula* menu. EXCEL automatically places the contents of the first cell in the range in the *Name:* text box, provided this is not a numerical value. Of course, you can change this name if you wish. In the *Refers To:* box you will see an absolute reference for the selected range.

Method:

1 Select the cell or range to which you want to assign a name.

2 Choose the *Define Name* command from the *Formula* menu.

3 Confirm the name in the *Name:* box, or give another name.

4 Confirm the reference in the *Refers To:* box, or give another reference (a reference always begins with an equal sign).

5 Confirm the dialog box by clicking on *OK*.

You can also use the *Define Name* dialog box to request a summary of names which have already been assigned or to change or erase a name or reference.

Exercise 18

1 Load the EXAMP2.XLS worksheet.

2 Enter the following in the dialog box:

Name: text box	*Refers To:* text box
Total_turnover	$E$10
Branch_turnover	$E$6:$E$9

3 Save the result using *File - Save*.

Assigning a name to a value or a formula
EXCEL also offers the possibility of assigning a name to a value or formula without having to use a cell. For example, it is possible to assign the name 'provisional' to the 3% commission percentage. You can change this afterwards and, if you do so, all the formulas in the worksheet where the corresponding name is used will automatically be recalculated.

Method:

1   Choose the *Define Name* command from the *Formula* menu.

2   Type the desired name in the *Name:* text box.

3   Fill in the value or formula in the *Refers To:* box, after the equal sign (=).

4   Click on *OK*.

Create Names
This command, from the *Formula* menu, uses the text in the columns or rows of a selected range to name the other cells in that range.

Method:

1   Select the range to be named including the text to be used as the name.

2   Choose the *Create Names* command from the *Formula* menu.

3   Make a choice from *Create Names In*.

4   Confirm the dialog box by clicking on *OK*.

Exercise 19

In the TOTWORLD.XLS worksheet, we want to name the cells containing the turnover totals for the three regions using the column name 'Total'.

1   Load the worksheet.

2   Select the range, including the column title.

3   Choose the *Create Names* command from the *Formula* menu.

4 Activate the top box *Top Row* and confirm by clicking on *OK*.

5 Check the result using *Formula - Define Name*.

Pasting a name

There are two ways to use names:

■ When entering a formula in the formula bar, you can give a name instead of a reference using the keyboard. This method is not recommended for long names because of the risk of making typing mistakes.

■ You can make use of the *Paste Name* command from the *Formula* menu. This is done as follows:

1 Enter the formula in the formula bar until you reach the place where the name is to be.

2 Choose the *Paste Name* command from the *Formula* menu.

3 From the list, choose the name to be pasted.

4 Confirm with *OK*.

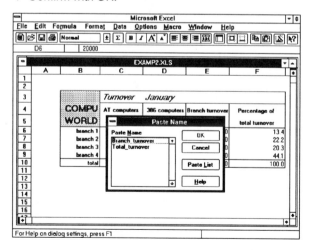

Exercise 20

1 Load worksheet EXAMP2.XLS.

2 Click in column F ('Percentage of total turnover') on the cell for the first branch (F6) and type an equal sign (=). This activates the formula bar.

3 Choose the *Formula - Paste Name* command and choose the name 'Branch_turnover' from the list. After you have confirmed the dialog box by clicking on OK, the name is pasted into the formula bar.

4 Continue typing, without spaces: *100/ and activate the *Formula - Paste Name* command again. This time, choose the name 'Total_turnover'. After confirming the dialog box with *OK*, confirm the formula with Enter. It now looks like this:

*Branch_turnover*100/Total_turnover*

Copy the formula using *Edit - Fill Down* to the previously selected range F7:F9.

Applying names
In worksheets where the formula contains mainly cell references rather than names, you can replace the cell references with names which you assign beforehand. You can do this using the *Formula - Apply Names* command.

For example, in a worksheet with an interest calculation, it is possible to assign the name 'Capital' to reference $B$4 and 'Interest' to $C$6. The *Formula - Apply Names* command then replaces the relevant references in the worksheet with the chosen names.

Method:

1 Select the range where the references are to be replaced by names. If only one cell is selected, EXCEL uses names throughout the worksheet instead of references.

2 Choose the *Formula - Apply Names* command.

3 From the list, choose the names to be used.

4 Switch on the *Ignore Relative/Absolute* check box.

5 Switch on the *Use Row and Column Names* check box.

6 Confirm the dialog box with *OK*.

The *Ignore Relative/Absolute* check box determines the reference format in your worksheet. As standard, EXCEL chooses an **absolute** reference format for names and a **relative** reference format for references in formulas. If you switch on the *Ignore Relative/Absolute* check box, EXCEL replaces the relevant references by the chosen names, irrespective of the format. When *Ignore Relative/Absolute* is switched off, absolute references are only replaced by absolute names, relative references by relative names and mixed references by mixed names.

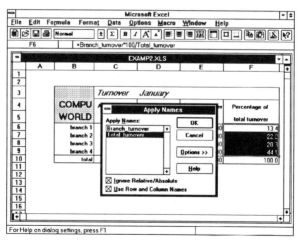

If the *Use Row and Column Names* check box is switched off, EXCEL *only* replaces the references for which you have already chosen a name. If you activate the box, EXCEL also tries to use a name for all other references. The program then uses row and column names.

Example:
Since the formulas in worksheet EXAMP1.XLS are already present, we could have performed Exercise 20 much more easily using the command *Formula - Apply Names* described here:

1 Load worksheet EXAMP2.XLS.

2 Select the range F6:F9 (percentages).

3 Choose the *Formula - Apply Names* command.

4 From the list, choose the name 'Branch_turnover'.

4 Click on *OK.*

7 Choose the *Formula - Apply Names* command.

8 From the list, choose the name 'Total_turnover'.

9 Click on *OK.*

The references in the formulas are then immediately replaced by the names.

2.9.2   Working with functions

The concept of a function
A function is a standardised formula which performs operations using values and produces the result of these operations in the form of a value. You can use functions individually as abbreviated formulas, but also as a module for simplifying large formulas.

A function consists of a **function name** with **arguments** in parentheses:

FUNCTIONNAME(arguments)

The first bracket comes immediately after the function name. The effect of the function is often recognisable from its name. A comma is used to separate arguments. EXCEL accepts numbers, text, logical values, matrices, error values and references as function arguments.

Example:

=SUM(B5:B20,C8,80)

Entering functions You can enter functions using the keyboard. As is usual for formulas, you must start with an equal sign (=). It makes no difference whether you use upper or lower case letters.

To avoid making typing mistakes, it is better to enter the required function using the *Paste Function* command from the *Formula* menu. A dialog box will then appear on the screen, which gives an alphabetical option list of all the available function categories. You can search the list for the required function, using the scroll bar or by typing in the initial letter. Paste the function by double-clicking or by confirming the dialog box by clicking on *OK* after you have selected the required function.

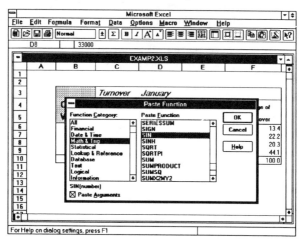

Method:

1   Select the cell where the formula is to be entered.

2   Choose the *Formula - Paste Function* command.

3   Choose a function from the list.

4   Activate the *Paste Arguments* box if you want to use placeholders for arguments in the formula.

5   Click on *OK*.

6   Give the arguments or replace the placeholders with the required arguments.

7   Confirm the formula with Enter or by clicking on the enter button.

Help in choosing a function

To prevent you losing sight of the profuse standard functions, EXCEL offers an excellent support system. By clicking on *Help* or pressing F1 you can call up the help system. The Contents include the *Worksheet Functions* option. Use this to request a list of all the available functions. Click on the desired function to display the relevant help text on the screen, containing information about the operation and syntax of the relevant functions. You will also find references to related functions, as well as examples.

Types of function

EXCEL's standard functions can be divided into the following groups:

- all worksheet functions (alphabetical list)
- financial functions
- date and time functions
- mathematical functions
- statistical functions
- lookup & reference functions
- database functions

- text functions
- logical functions
- information functions
- engineering functions.

This type of book cannot possibly cover all the functions and their corresponding arguments. Please refer to the above-mentioned help system for more detailed information concerning EXCEL functions. Here, we will deal with how to use functions in general, using a number of examples.

The statistical SUM function
In our first example (see worksheet EXAMP1.XLS) we had to calculate the turnover per branch for four columns. We did this using the formula B4+B5+B6+B7 in cell B8, in the 'AT computers' column.

In this case, entering the formula was no problem. But just imagine the formula if COMPUWORLD were to acquire sixty branches (B4+B5...B62+B63). It is a good idea to avoid using this type of formula because of its complexity, the high risk of making mistakes while entering the formula and the maximum limit of 255 characters. The SUM function offers an easier solution - SUM(B4:B7). If you use this, you can add and erase rows wherever you like between B4 and B7 without having to change the function argument.

In this example, we have given the range to be added as the argument. If you assign a name to the range (e.g. 'AT_turnover') you can also use this as the argument. The formula would then be: SUM(AT_turnover).

SUM also accepts multiple arguments. The formula SUM(C4:C8,C10:C15,B5,12) produces the sum of ranges C4:C8 and C10:C15, cell B5 and the value 12.

From version 3.0 onwards the *AutoSUM* button in the Toolbar can be used for addition. If you click on it, EXCEL automatically puts a SUM formula in the active cell with, as an argument, a reference to the adjacent range of numbers in the same column above the cell, or in the same row, to the left of the cell.

The IF logical function
In a worksheet we often have to deal with a problem where specific action has to be taken, depending on the contents of a cell. For example, if the quarterly turnover of one of the branches of COMPUWORLD is more than £500,000, the branch receives a turnover bonus of 3%.

This problem can be solved using the IF function. In global terms, our problem looks like this:

> **If** the contents of the Turnover cell is higher than £500,000
> **then** the result of Turnover/100*3 must appear in the Premium cell,
> **otherwise** the Premium cell has the value 0.

The syntax of the IF function is as follows:

IF(logical-test,value-if-true,value-if-false)

The result of the logical test determines the value produced by the IF function. If the result of the logical test is TRUE, the premium cell is given *value-as-true.* If the result of the logical test is FALSE, the Premium cell receives *value-as-false.*

*IF(quarterly_turnover>500,000,quarterly_turnover/ 100*3,0)*

It is possible to make nested loops of a maximum of seven IF functions. It is particularly important in such cases to have the brackets in the correct place. Imagine that COMPUWORLD works with increasing turnover premiums:

above £500,000	3%
£250,000 to £500,000	2%
£100,000 to £250,000	1%
£0 to £250,000	0%

The Premium Percentage cell would then be given the following formula:

IF(turnover>500000,3,IF(turnover>250000,2,IF(turn over>100000>,1,0)))

Using the result of this calculation, we can now work out the following in the Premium cell: turnover/100*premium_percentage.

Date and time functions
In date and time calculations, EXCEL uses serial numbers from 0 to 65380 for dates between 01-01-1900 and 31-12-2078. The figures in front of the point represent the date and those behind it, the time. A whole number represents a day (33604 = 01-01-1992). A decimal value represents the time (0.5 = 12/24 = 1200).

Using these numbers, calculations can be performed, such as computing due dates or the differences between two dates or times.

The NOW() function produces the current time and date as a serial number. This number is automatically given a date format. The function obtains this data from the computer's internal clock. You do not have to give any arguments, but the brackets are necessary.

On 21/09/1992 at 17:25 NOW() produces the serial number 33868.72628.
Summary of the number of letters in date and time formats:

code	meaning
D	day as number (1-31)
DD	day as number with possible pre-zero (01-31)
DDD	abbreviated day (Sun-Sat)

DDDD	day in full (Sunday-Saturday)
M	month as number (1-12)
MM	month as number with possible pre-zero (01-12)
MMM	abbreviated month (Jan-Dec)
MMMM	month in full (January-December)
YY	year as two-digit number (00-99)
YYYY	year as four-digit number (1900-2078)

If you choose the format 'DD-MMM-YY' for the previously mentioned cell, EXCEL changes the serial number into '21 Sep 92'. If you choose the 'D-M-YY.hh.mm' format, in addition to the date, you will also be given the time: '21-9-91 21.20'.

The DATE, DATEVALUE, TIME and TIMEVALUE functions allow you to convert data into serial numbers.

Example:

DATE(92,1,1) produces serial number 33604.

The DAY, WEEKDAY, MONTH, YEAR, HOUR, MINUTE and SECOND change the serial number into the value indicated by their name.

Examples:

DAY(33604) produces 1.
MONTH(33604) produces 1.
YEAR(33604) produces 1992. HOUR(0.8895) produces 21.

Using the functions indicated it is possible to work out the time difference in days between two dates. We will start a new worksheet and enter the current time and date in cell B2. To do this, we will use the NOW() function. In cell C2 type the due date, e.g. 30 May 1993.

current date	due date	number of days
01-01-93	31-05-93	150

We will calculate the difference between the two dates in cell D4 using the subtraction C2-B2.

Last example:

When planning routes, in order to calculate the time required, the following calculation has to be performed, amongst others:
start+days=finish

We shall assume that the start date is in cell B2 and has the format D-M-YY. The days are given as a whole number in cell D2. The addition B2+D2 in cell C2 produces the finish date as a serial number. If you choose a date format for this cell, such as 'DD MMMM YY', the date '17 January 1992' will appear in front of '1-1-92+16'.

2.9.3　Notes for cells and formulas

In order to simplify maintenance, all today's good programming systems are able to document programs using comments in the source text. Most database programs also offer documentation possibilities in the form of what are known as 'memo fields'. EXCEL enables you to add comments to a cell in the form of notes. This gives you an excellent way of saving, along with the worksheet, essential information about the operation of, and links within, a worksheet, so that this information is always available.

The Cell Note dialog box
To enter notes, you will use *Formula* - *Note* to open the dialog box shown in the illustration below.

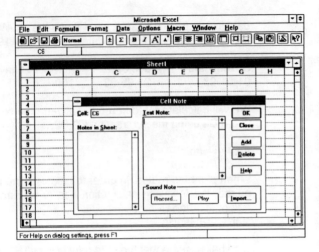

In the dialog box, you will see the *Cell:* text box. This contains the reference to the cell to which you want to add a note. The *Notes in Sheet:* list gives a summary of all the cells in the worksheet to which notes have already been added. In the *Text Note:* enter box, type the note you wish to add to the cell you have previously indicated. If you choose a note from the *Notes in Sheet:* list, the enter box shows the complete text and the *Cell:* text box shows the reference to the relevant cell. The buttons in the dialog box are self-explanatory.

You can drag the dialog box to anywhere on the screen using the mouse. This enables you to see the cells to which you want to add notes.

Adding and deleting notes
Method:

1 Select the cell to which a note is to be added.

2 Choose the *Note* option from the *Formula* menu.

3 Type text in the *Text Note:* box, without using Enter to start a new line.

4 Click on *OK*.

If you want to add notes to several cells, you must give the cell reference each time in the *Cell:* text box. Then type the note and click on the *Add* button.

To erase a note, choose the desired note from the list and click on the *Delete* button. Before EXCEL deletes the note, the program asks for confirmation.

Viewing and printing notes
You can call up the dialog box with the note whenever you wish using *Formula - Note.* It is also possible to view notes in the so-called Info window. This is opened by choosing the *Workspace* option from the *Options* menu. Then activate *Info Window* and click on *OK.* The menu bar also changes.

From the *Window* menu, choose the *Arrange* option. If you activate *Tiled,* the worksheet and Info windows are placed next to each other. If you find this screen division impractical, you can move a window by clicking on its title bar and dragging it. Dragging the window frame enables you to change the size of a window.

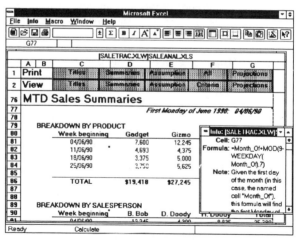

The contents of the Info window are defined using *Info.* Depending on your choice, in the window you will receive information about cells, formulas, values, formats, protection, names, source cells, target cells and notes.

If you then click on a cell in the worksheet window, you will receive the relevant information directly in the info window.

2.10   Questions and answers

Question 2-3: Distribution of profit

The owner of the company COMPUWORLD, Mr Big, is setting up a software development company together with Mr Bigger and Mr Lawson. They choose to make their company a trading partnership.

The three of them agree that each partner will initially receive 4% interest on the capital he contributed. The remaining profit will be shared equally. If the profit is insufficient to pay the interest or if the company is making a loss, the result will also be apportioned individually.

The distribution of profit is to be calculated using an EXCEL worksheet.

The problem must be solved using the following stages:

1   Enter the text and the numbers.

2   Enter the formulas to calculate the interest on contributed capital, individual payments, total profit share per partner and total profit distribution.

3   Format of numbers: £ before the number, a comma for separating thousands and two decimals.

4   Screen display: no gridlines, frame and shading as in the following illustration.

5 Print the worksheet.

6 Save the worksheet on the harddisk under the name COMPANY.XLS.

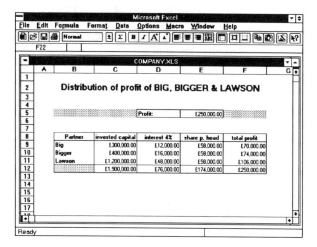

Question 2-4: Bill of exchange negotiation

Some of COMPUWORLD's customers often use a bill of exchange to settle their debts. Mr Macawber, COMPUWORLD's accountant, would therefore like to use an EXCEL worksheet to calculate the cash value of these bills of exchange. The worksheet must be suitable for calculating five bills of exchange.

Note:
Negotiated means that a bill of exchange is sold before its due date, after calculation of the discount rate. The cash value of the bill of exchange on the relevant day is calculated by deducting the bill's discount rate and costs from the value of the bill. Banks usually calculate a minimum discount rate and a minimum commission.

Information required

For each worksheet: minimum discount amount in £, commission in thousandths, minimum commission in £, date on which the cash value is to be calculated.

For each bill of exchange: discount in percent, exchange value, due date.

Values to be calculated: number of days from date of payment to due date, discount figure (#), discount amount, commission amount, cash value.

The following illustration shows the text for the worksheet, its format and the screen display settings.

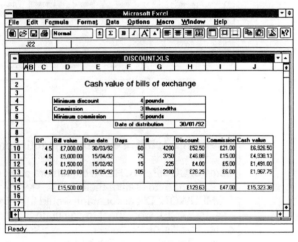

Save the worksheet as DISCOUNT.XLS.

Question 2-5: Comparison of depreciation methods

Retrogressive, linear and digital depreciation methods are to be compared in a worksheet. The purchase price is to be depreciated to a certain residual value. The worksheet must be able to show a maximum depreciation period of thirty years.

Retrogressive depreciation uses a maximum depreciation of 30 percent. However, we shall switch to linear depreciation as soon as the amount of depreciation for the remaining duration, using linear depreciation, is higher than for retrogressive depreciation.

Data to be entered: purchase price in pounds, residual value in pounds, depreciation period in years.

Print out the worksheet and then save it as DE-PREC.XLS.

The worksheet should look like this:

Microsoft Excel — DEPREC.XLS

	Purchase price		Residual value		Depreciation period	
		£250,000.00		£800.00		25

	Retrogressive depreciation		Linear depreciation		Digital depreciation	
Year	Depreciation	Residual value	Depreciation	Residual value	Depreciation	Residual value
1	£29,904.00	£220,096.00	£9,968.00	£240,032.00	£19,169.23	£230,830.77
2	£26,411.52	£193,684.48	£9,968.00	£230,064.00	£18,402.46	£212,428.31
3	£23,242.14	£170,442.34	£9,968.00	£220,096.00	£17,635.69	£194,792.62
4	£20,453.08	£149,989.26	£9,968.00	£210,128.00	£16,868.92	£177,923.69
5	£17,998.71	£131,990.55	£9,968.00	£200,160.00	£16,102.15	£161,821.54
6	£15,838.87	£116,151.68	£9,968.00	£190,192.00	£15,335.38	£146,486.15
7	£13,938.20	£102,213.48	£9,968.00	£180,224.00	£14,568.62	£131,917.54
8	£12,265.62	£89,947.86	£9,968.00	£170,256.00	£13,801.85	£118,115.69
9	£10,793.74	£79,154.12	£9,968.00	£160,288.00	£13,035.08	£105,080.62
10	£9,498.49	£69,655.63	£9,968.00	£150,320.00	£12,268.31	£92,812.31
11	£8,358.68	£61,296.95	£9,968.00	£140,352.00	£11,501.54	£81,310.77
12	£7,355.63	£53,941.32	£9,968.00	£130,384.00	£10,734.77	£70,576.00

Ready

Answer to question 2-3

a) After entering the text and the contributed capital per partner, we can define the following names:

cell $E$5	profit

range $C$9:$C$11	capital
range $D$9:$D$11	interest
range $E$9:$E$11	share
range $F$9:$F$11	total

b) Formulas:
Provided there are sufficient profits, interest is calculated using 'capital/100*4'. That is why a test must be carried out:

IF(SUM(capital/100*4)<=profit,capital/100*4,0)

This formula will be placed in cell D9 and will then be copied to D10 and D11.

To calculate the share per head '(profit-SUM(interest))/3' the remaining profit from 'profit-SUM(interest)' must be greater than 0.

Otherwise, the partners receive nothing per head and, if the company is making a loss, the 'Share per head' column shows the sum which must be made up.

This looks like this, as a formula:

IF(profit-SUM(interest)>0,(profit-SUM(interest))/3,IF(profit>0,0,profit/3))

This formula is intended for cell E9. Then copy it to cells E10 and E11.

The total profit per partner is calculated using interest+share in cell F9. This formula is then copied to F10 and F11.

Finally, the totals in row 12 are to be calculated. The formulas for this are:

C12: SUM(capital)
D12: SUM(interest)
E12: SUM(share)
F12: SUM(total)

Answer to question 2-4

a) The question and the corresponding illustration contain the data (text, numbers and format) you require.

The following names have to be defined:

minimum discount	md	$F$4
commission percentage	comm	$F$5
minimum commission	mincomm	$F$6
date of distribution	disdat	$H$7
discount percentage	dp	C10:C14
bill value	bv	D10:D14
due date	duedat	E10:E14
number of days	days	F10:F14
discount figure	df	G10:G14
discount amount	da	H10:H14
commission amount	ca	I10:I14
cash value	cv	J10:J14

b) Formulas have to be developed for calculating the number of days between the date of distribution and the due date, the discount figure, the commission and the cash value. Enter these formulas in the cells of row ten and then copy them to the cells in rows 11 to 14 inclusive. The cells in columns E to J and rows 10 to 14 can only contain a value if an amount is given for the bill value in the relevant rows of column D. Generally, the following applies to these cells:

IF(bv>0,calculate value,"")

Switch off the *Zero Values* check box in the *Options - Display* dialog box.

We can now give the following formulas:

1   To calculate the number of days, the financial
    year is used (1 month = 30 days, 1 year = 360
    days). We will use date function DAYS360():

    DAYS360(disdat,duedat)

2   The discount figure (#) is the rounded off whole
    figure from the calculation 'bill_value/100*days',
    i.e.:

    IF(bv>0,ROUND(TRUNC(bv/100*days,0),0),"")

3   When calculating the discount amount, we must
    remember that the calculated amount must be
    higher than the minimum discount, i.e.:

    IF(bv>0,if((df/(360/dp))<md,md,df/(360/dp)),"")

4   The   commission   is   calculated   using
    'bill_value/1000*commission_percentage'. If the
    result is lower than the minimum commission,
    this is then used, i.e.:

    IF(bv>0,if(bv/1000*comm<mincomm,
    mincomm,bv/1000*comm),"")

5   To calculate the cash value we must deduct the
    discount and commission from the bill value, i.e.:

    IF(bv>0,bv-da-ca,0)

6   For the additions in row 15, use the SUM func-
    tion:

    SUM(bv)
    SUM(da)
    SUM(ca)
    SUM(cv)

Answer to question 2-5

a) First, copy the texts and the format from the illustration in the question.

Then define the following names:

purchase price	pp	$E$2
residual value	rv	$H$2
depreciation period	per	$K$2
year	year	B8:B37
retrogressive depreciation percentage	p	

The name p does not have a reference linked to it, instead it has the following formula:

IF((100/per)*3>30,30,(100/per)*3)

b) Now we deal with the formulas, that for retrogressive depreciation first, where the depreciation amount of the residual value is always calculated using a constant percentage.

1   The highest retrogressive depreciation percentage is the linear percentage multiplied by three, but with a maximum of 30 percent, i.e.:

IF((100/per)*3>30,30,(100/per)*3)

We have already assigned this formula to the name p.

2   The depreciation percent for the first year then amounts to:

((pp-rv)/100)*p

3   In cell E8, the residual value for the first year is calculated using:

pp-D8

4   The ROW() function produces the row number.
     By repeatedly reducing the result of this function
     by 7 we can number the years in column B.

     The table is designed for a depreciation period
     of a maximum of 30 years. If the period is shor-
     ter, we only want to display the relevant number
     of rows in the table. This is why all the cells in
     rows 8 to 37 must conform to the following basic
     pattern:

     IF(ROW()-7>per,"",calculate_values)

     Enter the following formula in cell B8 and then
     copy it down to cell B37:

     IF(ROW()-7>per,"",ROW()-7)

5   As a result of the switch from retrogressive to li-
     near, when calculating the depreciation amount
     for the following years, this applies:

     if   residual value/residual duration > retro-
           gressive depreciation amount
           then calculate linear depreciation amount
           otherwise calculate retrogressive depreci-
           ation amount

     Where:
     residual duration = per-year+1
     retrogressive depreciation amount = residual
     value/100*p
     linear depreciation amount = residual value/
     (per-year+1)

     Using these data we can put the following for-
     mula into cell D9, and copy this down sub-
     sequently to cell D37 inclusive.

     IF(ROW()-7>per,"",IF((E8-rv)/(per-year+1)>
     *(E8-rv)/100*p,(E8- rv)/(per-year+1),E8/100*p))*

6   The residual values are calculated by deducting
    the depreciation amount from the residual value
    for the previous year. Enter the following formula
    in cell E9 and copy it down to cell E37 inclusive:

IF(ROW()-7>per,"",E8-D9)

7   Now come the formulas for calculating the linear
    depreciation. Here, all depreciation amounts are
    the same.

    You can simplify your work by using the stand-
    ard function SLN (Straight-Line Depreciation),
    which EXCEL makes available for calculating li-
    near depreciations. The syntax is as follows:
    SLN(costs,residual_value,duration).

    Specify as arguments:

    costs   purchase value
    residual value
    duration   the period for which deprecia-
                      tion is calculated

    The formula for the range G8:G37 looks like this:

IF(ROW()-7>per,"",SLN(pp,rv,per))

8   To calculate the residual value at the end of the
    first year, cell H8 is to contain this formula:

IF(ROW)-7>per,"",pp-g8)

    Cell H9 is to contain the formula for subsequent
    years:

IF(ROW)-7>per,"",h8-g9)

    Copy this formula down to cell H37 inclusive.

9   To calculate the digital depreciation amounts,
    we use the so-called Sum of Years' Digits

method. For this purpose, EXCEL provides the standard SYD functions. The syntax is as follows:

SYD(costs,residual_value,duration,per). The function produces the digital depreciation amount for the year specified as 'per'. The other arguments are the same as for SLN. The formula for cell J8 is therefore:

IF(ROW()-7>per,"",SYD(pp,rv,per,ROW()-7))

Copy this formula down to cell J37 inclusive.

10 The formulas for calculating the residual value are included in 8.

DEPREC.XLS

Purchase price	£250,000.00	Residual value	£800.00	Depreciation period	25

	Retrogressive depreciation		Linear depreciation		Digital depreciation	
Year	Depreciation	Residual value	Depreciation	Residual value	Depreciation	Residual value
1	£29,904.00	£220,096.00	£9,968.00	£240,032.00	£19,169.23	£230,830.77
2	£26,411.52	£193,684.48	£9,968.00	£230,064.00	£18,402.46	£212,428.31
3	£23,242.14	£170,442.34	£9,968.00	£220,096.00	£17,635.69	£194,792.62
4	£20,453.08	£149,989.26	£9,968.00	£210,128.00	£16,868.92	£177,923.69
5	£17,998.71	£131,990.55	£9,968.00	£200,160.00	£16,102.15	£161,821.54
6	£15,838.87	£116,151.68	£9,968.00	£190,192.00	£15,335.38	£146,486.15
7	£13,938.20	£102,213.48	£9,968.00	£180,224.00	£14,568.62	£131,917.54
8	£12,265.62	£89,947.86	£9,968.00	£170,256.00	£13,801.85	£118,115.69
9	£10,793.74	£79,154.12	£9,968.00	£160,288.00	£13,035.08	£105,080.62
10	£9,498.49	£69,655.63	£9,968.00	£150,320.00	£12,268.31	£92,812.31
11	£8,358.66	£61,296.95	£9,968.00	£140,352.00	£11,501.54	£81,310.77
12	£7,355.63	£53,941.32	£9,968.00	£130,384.00	£10,734.77	£70,576.00
13	£6,472.96	£47,468.36	£9,968.00	£120,416.00	£9,968.00	£60,608.00
14	£5,696.20	£41,772.16	£9,968.00	£110,448.00	£9,201.23	£51,406.77
15	£5,012.66	£36,759.50	£9,968.00	£100,480.00	£8,434.46	£42,972.31
16	£4,411.14	£32,348.36	£9,968.00	£90,512.00	£7,667.69	£35,304.62
17	£3,881.80	£28,466.55	£9,968.00	£80,544.00	£6,900.92	£28,403.69
18	£3,458.32	£25,008.24	£9,968.00	£70,576.00	£6,134.15	£22,269.54
19	£3,458.32	£21,549.92	£9,968.00	£60,608.00	£5,367.38	£16,902.15
20	£3,458.32	£18,091.60	£9,968.00	£50,640.00	£4,600.62	£12,301.54
21	£3,458.32	£14,633.28	£9,968.00	£40,672.00	£3,833.85	£8,467.69
22	£3,458.32	£11,174.96	£9,968.00	£30,704.00	£3,067.08	£5,400.62
23	£3,458.32	£7,716.64	£9,968.00	£20,736.00	£2,300.31	£3,100.31
24	£3,458.32	£4,258.32	£9,968.00	£10,768.00	£1,533.54	£1,566.77
25	£3,458.32	£800.00	£9,968.00	£800.00	£766.77	£800.00

Page 1

3   Charts

We now come to the field of business graphics, and the
opportunities provided by EXCEL for the layout and
presentation of figures. Based on the motto, "a picture is
worth more than a thousand words", this branch of
graphic layout deals with presenting large quantities of
figures in a clear, uncomplicated way so that mutual re-
lationships or differences can be seen at a glance.

Business graphics are becoming an increasingly important resource in decision-making, planning and control in a wide range of fields. In graphic displays, the
preferred chart formats are bar charts, area charts, pie
charts, xy (scatter) charts and line charts.

3.1   Basic skills for working with charts

In EXCEL, a chart is a graphic representation of worksheet data, which is why there is always a close link between the **chart** file and the worksheet file which is the
source of the values in the chart. Worksheet files have
an .XLS extension, and chart files have the extension
.XLC (C for Chart). EXCEL offers you the choice of fourteen different types of chart, each one with varying format possibilities.

Before you create a chart, we shall first explain a few
basic techniques.

EXCEL manages a chart within a **chart window**. This
window can be distinguished from a worksheet window
by its different menu bar. In terms of operation, however, both windows are the same.

The illustration below shows the most important elements of a chart window:

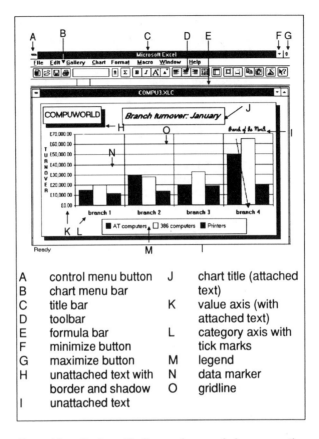

A	control menu button	J	chart title (attached text)
B	chart menu bar		
C	title bar	K	value axis (with attached text)
D	toolbar		
E	formula bar	L	category axis with tick marks
F	minimize button		
G	maximize button	M	legend
H	unattached text with border and shadow	N	data marker
		O	gridline
I	unattached text		

Everything displayed in the workspace is known as the **chart**. The **plot area** is the most important part of the chart. This is the area defined by axes where the values are displayed.

Axes serve as reference lines for representing values in charts. EXCEL distinguishes between the **category axis** (often the horizontal axis) and the **value axis** (often the vertical axis) .

It is possible to place text alongside the axes and to choose from four different writing directions. As standard, EXCEL puts **tick marks** along both axes. **Tick labels** define the tick marks. The **gridlines** run horizontally or vertically through the plot area.

A **data marker** represents a value from the worksheet. In bar charts, the bars are the data markers, in line charts they are marked by lines and in scatter charts, dots or small symbols. Data markers which are related to each other form a **chart data series** (e.g. bars of the same colour). The data markers in the data series are the same colour, the same pattern or the same symbol. Obviously, colours can only be used in a chart if you have a computer with a colour screen. On monochrome screens, individual data series can also be clearly recognised because EXCEL shows them in different shades of grey or with different patterns. A data series is made up of values from the worksheet which together form a category. These values are defined using a **series formula**.

Text can be attached to the various elements of the chart. If you move an element, the relevant text automatically moves with it. This is why it is called **attached text**. The opposite of this, **unattached text**, can be moved around as required within the chart.

The legend shows which colour, pattern or symbol has been used to display the individual data series, where the series can be recognised by a series name.

3.2   Creating a new chart

3.2.1   Selecting values

We are going to use known figures for our first chart. Start EXCEL and load the EXAMP3.XLS worksheet. This is the result of exercise 16. The illustration below shows this worksheet:

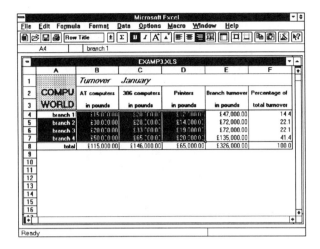

We want the chart we are going to create to show the turnover of the four branches for each of the three product groups.

To do this, you must select the required values from the worksheet. As you can see from the illustration, this concerns the range A4:D7. The text immediately above and/or beside the value range to be selected can also be selected for use as axis labels in the chart. However, in our example only the names of the branches need to be selected with the values. Start selecting at cell A4 and drag the mouse diagonally to cell D7. You have now selected the values for the chart.

3.2.2   Creating a chart

Now open the *File* menu, click on *New* and choose the *Chart* option in the dialog box, by double-clicking.

EXCEL opens the chart window with the required chart.

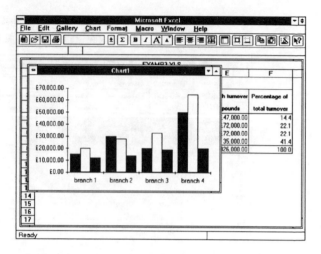

The chart window is now the active window. You can tell this from the changed menu bar and the dark title bar with the temporary file name 'Chart1'.

As standard, EXCEL chooses to display a new chart as a bar chart. The scale is chosen on the basis of the relevant maximum and minimum values so that the space available in the work area is used in an optimum manner. EXCEL works out a sensible graduated scale for the value axis.

In the previous example, the names of the four branches have been copied from the worksheet to be used as labels for the category axis of the chart. The three bars of a category show the turnover for a branch in the three product groups. Bars with the same pattern are part of the same data series. Therefore, our chart is based on three data series: 'AT computers', 386 computers' and 'Printers'.

Now we want to make another chart. Click the mouse on the EXAMP3.XLS window. The menu bar changes again and the worksheet window is active again, overlaid on the chart window. First, undo any selections by clicking in any cell.

Two ranges are now to be selected, in this case B2:D2 and A4:D7. You can make this multiple selection by dragging the mouse across cells B2:D2, then A4:D7, while holding the Ctrl key down. After you have selected the first range, release the left mouse button.

After *File - New* and choosing *Chart*, a second chart window appears, called 'Chart2'.

This time, EXCEL has created a category for each of the three product groups, showing the turnover of the four branches.

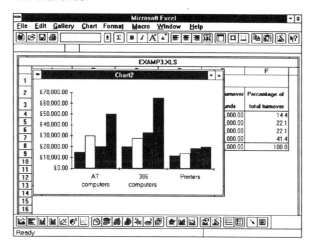

EXCEL also enables charts to be included in a work-sheet. After selecting the range for the chart (in this case B2:D2 and B4:D7), click on the *ChartWizard* tool (second from the right) in the Toolbar. A marker frame appears around the selected range and the cursor changes into a small cross hair. Move this to where you want the top left-hand corner of the chart to be. Then drag the mouse to the bottom right-hand corner of the range for the chart. When you release the left mouse button, a dialog box will appear offering various charting options. Click on *Next*. Make a selection and click again on *Next*. At the conclusion of the final step, click on *OK*.

EXCEL incorporates the chart as a drawing in the worksheet.

There is also a second possibility to include a chart in a worksheet. Click on *Options* and choose *Toolbars*. Then choose *Chart* and click on *Show*. A toolbar will appear at the bottom of the screen. If you then select a range, you can click on one of the buttons in this bar. A marker frame appears around the selected range and the cursor changes into a small cross hair. Move this to where you want the top left-hand corner of the chart to be. Then drag the mouse to the bottom right-hand corner of the new chart range. When you release the left mouse button the chart will be drawn in the worksheet.

Within the chart, the mouse pointer changes into an arrow. You can move the chart by clicking and dragging the pointer. The chart is marked with black squares. If you click on them, you can change the size of the chart horizontally, vertically or diagonally.

If you double-click on the chart, EXCEL opens a separate window where you can edit the chart.

3.2.3   Screen division possibilities

Within the EXCEL application window there are now three windows of differing sizes, partially or entirely overlaid on top of each other. You can open more windows, i.e. load worksheet or chart files, until you exceed the RAM capacity. Every window which is wholly or partially visible can be activated by clicking inside it using the mouse. Click on the maximize button to make the active window full-screen sized. The other windows are then, of course, completely hidden.

So how do we go about monitoring how many windows are open and how do we make them visible, either individually or together? The *Window* menu is useful in this respect. The command *Arrange* attempts to arrange all the document windows in such a way that a portion of each window remains visible.

However, you can also arrange the windows in a different way, altering both the height and width of the windows. If you click on the title bar you will then be able to drag the relevant window across the screen, holding down the left mouse button. You can change the size of a window by moving the frame edges or corners.

At the bottom of the *Window* menu, you will see a list, which can contain the names of a maximum of nine open windows. To choose a window from the list, click on its name. The relevant window is then displayed in full-screen size and is therefore overlaid on all the others. If more than nine windows are open, you can use the *More Windows* command to call up a dialog box containing an option list of all the open windows.

The *Hide* command hides an open window. The window is still loaded but remains invisible until it is activated again, using *Unhide.*

Exercise 21

By moving and changing the window size, try to create this arrangement of windows EXAMP3.XLS, Chart1 and Chart2:

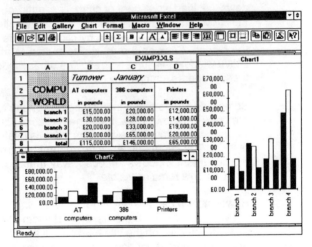

You can now see clearly that you can determine how the chart is drawn, using the *value* selection. In Chart1, the rows (branches) are the starting point for creating the categories, while in Chart2 it is the columns (products). The data series in Chart1 are compiled from the product groups and in Chart2 from the branches.

3.2.4   Defining data series

When defining a data series, EXCEL first checks whether the selected cells in the first row or column contain text for the category or value axis. EXCEL always tries to generate fewer data series than categories, which is why it then looks in the selected range to see whether data series have to be compiled per row or per column.

■ If the selected range (without series or category

names) is wider than it is high, or if the length and width are equal, EXCEL compiles the data series from the rows.
■ If the selected range (without series or category names) is higher than it is wide, EXCEL compiles the data series from the columns.

3.2.5 Elements of series formulas

Once compiled in this way, EXCEL converts the data series into series formulas, which form the basis of the chart. You can view these series formulas in the formula bar, by clicking on a data marker (e.g. a bar) in the chart window.

In Chart2, click on the category 2 data marker belonging to the third data series. All data markers forming part of this data series are now marked. You can see this by the white squares in the corresponding data markers. 'S3' appears at the top left of the formula bar. This is the series number for the selected series. The series formula comes after it:

SERIES(EXAMP3.XLS!$A$6,EXAMP3.XLS!$B$2:$ D$2,EXAMP3.XLS!$B$6:$D$6,3)

This kind of formula consists of the SERIES function name and four arguments between brackets:

SERIES(name_reference,categories,values,plot_order)

■ The argument *name_reference* is the name of the data series. This can be an external reference to a cell, an external name or text in inverted commas. In the previous example, the argument EXAMP3.XLS!$A$6 refers to the name 'branch 3' in cell A6 of worksheet EXAMP3.XLS. The exclamation mark (!) between the file name and the absolute reference is essential.
■ The *categories* argument uses an external reference to refer to the cells with the text for the category axis.

■ The *values* argument uses an external reference to refer to the range containing the values for the chart. In our example, this is B6:D6 of worksheet EXAMP3.XLS.

■ The *plot order* argument (always a whole number) determines the position of the data series in the chart. In our example, it is the third data series.

Exercise 22

It is also possible to edit series formulas. We are going to try this now by changing the reference
EXAMP3.XLS!$B$2:$D$2 into
EXAMP3.XLS!$B$3:$D$3 in all data series.

After you have confirmed the changed formula, EXCEL places the words 'in pounds' under the category axis.

This is clear proof of the link between the worksheet and the chart. We can also illustrate this link in another way. Click on worksheet EXAMP3.XLS and select cell B4 (turnover of AT computers for branch 1). Change the value 15,000 into 80,000 and watch what happens in the chart. As you can see, the corresponding data marker is immediately adapted to the changed value. To return to the original situation, put the old value back into the worksheet.

3.3   Saving and loading charts

Saving and loading a chart is just like saving or loading a worksheet. However, there is an important difference between the commands *Close, Save* and *Save As* in the *File* menu.

Activate the Chart2 window and choose the *File - Close* command. After you have answered no to whether the changes have to be saved, the chart disappears from the screen and no longer exists (not even on the hard-disk).

We will not do this with Chart1 because we want to continue working with it. Activate the relevant window and
choose the *File - Save As* command. Change the name
Chart1 into COMPU3 and confirm with *OK*. EXCEL
automatically gives the file the extension .XLC and
saves it in the current directory on the harddisk. If you
want to save the file in another directory, you must
choose the required directory from the list.

We had already saved worksheet EXAMP3.XLS. We
only need to save it again using *File - Save* if the file has
been changed since the last time it was saved and if the
new version is to replace the old one. If you do not want
to do this, remove the worksheet from the screen using
the *Close* command from the *File* menu, or save it again
under another name.

If you want to close several worksheets and charts at
the same time, open the *File* menu, while holding down
the Shift key. This changes the *Close* command into
Close All.

If you load a chart without first having loaded the corresponding worksheet, EXCEL asks if changes have to
be made to non-opened documents. You can usually
answer yes to this question.

To sum up, the Chart2 window has disappeared. The
chart in the Chart1 window has been saved as
COMPU3.XLC and is on the screen with worksheet
EXAMP3.XLS.

3.4 Printing charts

Printing a chart is also more or less the same as printing
a worksheet, with the exception that you cannot define
a print range in order to print only part of a chart.

However, the dialog box generated by the *File - Page
Setup* command does contain a number of other elements:

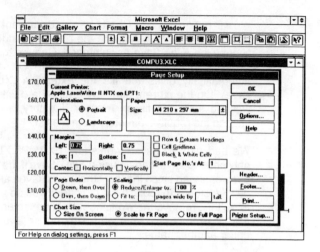

Three setup possibilities have been added at the bottom, for defining the format of the chart to be printed:

Size on Screen. The chart will be printed the same size as it appears on the screen.

Scale to Fit Page. The chart will be printed as large as possible with the same height/width ratio as on the screen.

Use Full Page. The chart will be printed so that it fills the whole page. This may mean that the original height/width ratio is considerably altered.

Operation:

1   If several printers are installed, choose the desired printer using the *File - Page Setup - Printer Setup* command.

2   Activate the window containing the chart which you want to print.

3   Specify the headers and footers, set the margins and define the format using *File - Page Setup.*

4 Choose the *Print Preview* command from the *File* menu, to get an impression of what the printout will look like on paper.

5 Repeat stage 3, if required, to change the chart.

6 Start printing by clicking on *OK* in the *File - Print* dialog box.

Exercise 23

Print out the COMPU3.XLC chart using the page setup *Scale to Fit Page*.

3.5 Types of chart

EXCEL displays charts as standard in the form of column charts. This is the **preferred type**. In addition to this type, there are ten other types of charts, each offering a choice of various formats. You can choose the required type of chart from the *Gallery* menu:

■ Area
■ Bar
■ Column
■ Line
■ Pie
■ Radar
■ XY (Scatter)
■ Combination
■ 3-D Area
■ 3-D Bar
■ 3-D Column
■ 3-D Line
■ 3-D Pie
■ 3-D Surface

For example, if you choose *Column* a dialog box appears, containing a choice of ten different formats for this type of chart:

1 simple column chart
2 column chart for one data series with varied colours or patterns
3 stacked column chart
4 overlapped column chart
5 100% stacked column chart
6 column chart with horizontal gridlines
7 column chart with value labels
8 step chart (no space between categories)
9 stacked with lines connecting data in the same series
10 100% stacked with lines connecting data in the same series

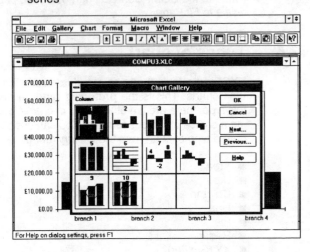

After double-clicking on one of these icons, your chart is immediately displayed in the form you have chosen. You can call up the formats for the other types of charts by clicking on *Next* or *Previous*. A summary of these types is given in Appendix E.

Exercise 24

Try out the various possibilities using the COMPU3.XLC file. This will give you an impression of the many types of charts EXCEL offers. When you have finished, you can restore the original chart type using the *Preferred* command from the *Gallery* menu.

3.6 Editing charts

Using the COMPU3.XLC chart, we shall demonstrate how to adapt the format of your chart, after you have chosen its type, to suit your personal requirements, by adding text and legends and using special formats.

If you have quit EXCEL, start the program again and load the COMPU3.XLC chart.

3.6.1 Parts of a chart and categories

EXCEL's formatting possibilities influence the various parts of a chart. EXCEL has the following categories of chart parts:

- chart
- plot area
- 3-D floor
- 3-D walls
- 3-D corners
- legends
- axes
- text
- arrows
- gridlines
- first data series
- second data series, etc.
- drop lines
- hi-lo lines
- up/down bars
- series lines

You can select categories and parts from this list using the cursor keys. To do this, use:

Cursor up	the first part of the following category
Cursor down	the last part of the previous category
Cursor right	the next part of the same category
Cursor left	the previous part of the same category

Simply click with the mouse on the required part.

Selected parts are marked with small squares. If these are black, you can move the relevant part or change their size using the mouse. If the squares are white, these operations are not possible.

3.6.2   Adding attached text

a) Entering text

Let's start with the title of the chart, which is: 'Branch turnover: January'.

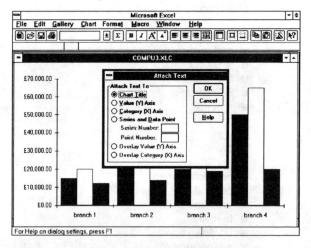

Choose the *Chart - Attach Text* command. The dialog box shows a summary of attached text elements. Attached text stays permanently with the element to which you assigned it. Its position is also permanent. You cannot therefore move attached text. The choice you make in this dialog box determines the position of the text in the chart.

When you have clicked on *Chart Title* followed by *OK*, the word 'Title', marked with white squares, appears at the top of the chart where the final title will be. In the formula bar, replace the standard text with 'Branch turnover: January' and confirm what you have entered. EXCEL now places the text in the chart as its title.

Note:
If the title is long, you can break off a line using Ctrl-Enter. Once the text has been entered, it can be formatted in the usual way after activating the formula bar.

The format of the title can be determined using the *Patterns, Font* and *Text* commands from the *Format* menu, in the same way as other attached text elements. Once you have activated one of the three commands, you also have access to the dialog boxes for the other two, without having to go back to the *Format* menu.

It is important to select the text to be formatted before choosing the first command.

b) Formatting text

Aligning text. Select the chart title by double-clicking on its name and choose the *Format - Text* command. You can determine the alignment and position of the text in the corresponding dialog box. We shall leave the standard setting as it is.

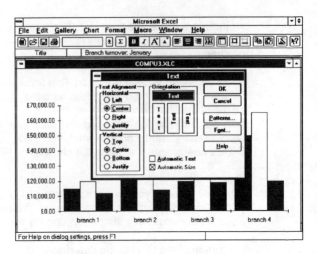

Using the *Patterns* command from the *Format* menu,
you can place a border around the title. However, you
do not need to close the *Text* dialog box to choose this
command, since you can switch directly to *Patterns*
using the relevant button.

Choosing a border. You specify the border in the left-
hand section of the dialog box on your screen. The
style, the **colour** and the **weight** of the border are
defined here. If you change these settings, the *Custom*
option button is automatically switched on. By clicking
on *Automatic* you can restore the original settings. If
you do not want a border around the text, choose *None.*
To put shadow around the border, check the *Shadow*
box.

The *Area* section in the dialog box enables you to specify colours or patterns for the area within the border.
You can choose both foreground and background colours. The foreground colour is assigned to the pattern,
and the background colour to the area within the border.
Choose the *Automatic* option from *Border* for the moment.

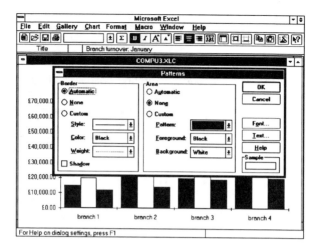

Choosing fonts. It is also possible to specify the **font, size, style, colour** and **background** of the text. You can do this using the *Font* command from the *Format* menu. You can also switch directly to this menu from the *Border* dialog box. However, to be able to change the type style, the title must first be selected.

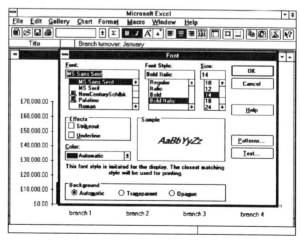

In the dialog box, choose the MS Sans Serif font, size

14 and the styles bold and italic. We have now finished formatting the chart title.

Note:
The *Opaque* background option, fills in the text background in white, or the chosen background colour. The background option *Transparent* leaves the original background colour as it was.

Operation:

1 Choose the attached text elements using *Chart - Attach Text.*

2 Type the desired text and confirm what you have entered.

3 To format the text, proceed to step 4, or end.

4 Select the text element.

5 **Text Alignment** using the *Format - Text* command. Settings:
   a) Horizontally: Left, Center, Right, Justify.
   b) Vertically: Top, Center, Bottom, Justify.

6 **Border** or **area** using the *Format - Patterns* command.
   a) You can specify Style, Color, Weight or Shadow for the border.
   b) You can specify Pattern, Foreground and Background for the area within the border.

7 **Format text** using the *Format - Font* command.
   a) Font
   b) Size (8, 10 etc.)
   c) Style (bold, italics etc.)
   d) Colour

Exercise 25

As you will realise from the *Chart - Attach Text* dialog box, the text for the axes is also attached text. Now try to place the text 'TURNOVER' vertically alongside the value axis and choose MS Sans Serif, size 8, bold and no border.

Remember to save the result using *File - Save.*

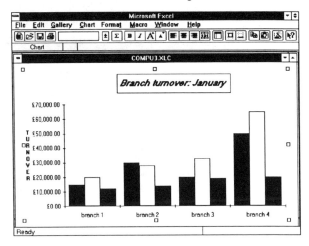

Note:
The other attached text elements are text for the category axis, text for series and data points and text for the overlay axes. These texts are automatically included in the chart via the series formulas, but they are not yet formatted.

3.6.3 Adding a legend

The *Add Legend* command from the *Chart* menu places a legend in the chart. These legends show which colours or patterns have been used for the individual data series. After the colour or pattern, you will see the name of the relevant data series, provided this has been co-

pied from the worksheet. EXCEL automatically puts a
frame around a legend. After it has been activated, the
Add Legend command from the *Chart* menu changes
into *Delete Legend* so that you can erase a legend. In
the *Format - Legend* dialog box you will see a choice of
four different locations for the position of the legend. As
standard, EXCEL places the legend to the right of the
chart.

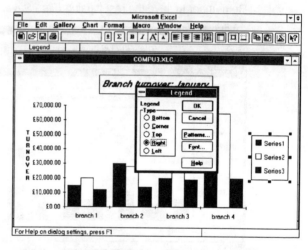

We want to place the legend at the bottom. After
double-clicking on the relevant button, you will see that
the legend has moved. Unfortunately, the names of the
data series are missing. We shall quickly rectify that
situation now. Click on the first data marker (left-hand
bar). The series formula appears in the formula bar. In
inverted commas and after the open bracket, type the
text 'AT computers' as the first argument. Click on the
next data marker and enter the text, again in inverted
commas, '386 computers'. Give the name 'Printers' to
the third data series. As you can see, these names are
immediately incorporated into the legend.

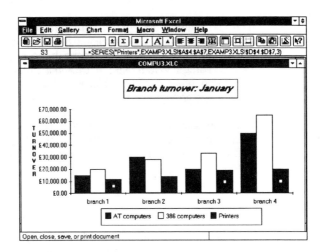

You can use the formatting possibilities discussed earlier for the legend too, by calling up the windows *Patterns* or *Fonts* from the *Format - Legend* dialog box.

Note:
When you select the legend, EXCEL marks it with black squares. This means that it is theoretically an unattached element. It is also possible therefore to move the legend at will by clicking inside it with the mouse and dragging it to the required position. You can also change the size of the legend by clicking on one of the black squares and moving it.

3.6.4 Adding unattached text

Unlike attached text, unattached text can be inserted anywhere in the chart. When entering unattached text, there must be no selected chart parts. Simply start typing; the formula bar is automatically activated.

You can also break off a line using Ctrl-Enter to begin a new line and you can edit the text later in the formula bar.

The text entered appears in the chart, surrounded by black squares, after confirmation using Enter or clicking on the enter box. You can now move the text by clicking on it and dragging it. Be sure to click in the middle of the text frame, otherwise you will activate the nearest black square and change the size of the text frame.

You can also apply the formatting possibilities discussed earlier to unattached text, by selecting the text and choosing the desired command from the *Format* menu.

Exercise 26

1 Type the text 'Branch of the Month'. Place this text above the bars for branch 4. For the text, choose font Script and size 12.

2 Type the company name 'COMPUWORLD'. Move this to the top left-hand corner of the chart and put a shadow around the text frame. Choose MS Sans Serif type style, size 14.

3 Save the result using the File - Save command.

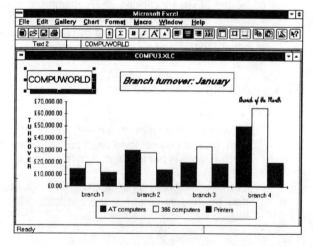

3.6.5 Adding an arrow

It is possible, using arrows, to emphasise particular sections of a chart. The arrow is an unattached element. You can place an arrow in your chart using *Chart - Add Arrow*.

After you have activated this command, an arrow appears in the chart, marked with three black squares. If you hold down the left mouse button, you can drag the arrow to the place you want it. The length and direction of the arrow are changed by moving the squares.

Provided the arrow is marked, it can be erased. You can only add subsequent arrows if no other arrows are selected.

The *Format - Patterns* command has a special dialog box for formatting an arrow, where you define the shape of the line and the arrow head.

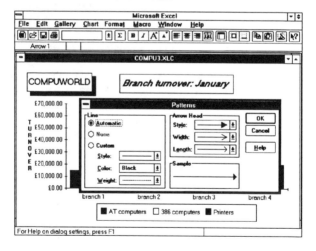

Exercise 27

Add an arrow to the COMPU3.XLC chart, pointing from the 'Branch of the Month' text to 'branch 4' on the category axis. For formatting the arrow, choose the same settings as those in the above illustration and save the result using *File - Save*.

3.6.6   Formatting charts and the plot area

On colour screens in particular, good optical effects can be achieved by formatting the plot area. A frame is to be placed around both the entire chart and the plot area. From the *Chart* menu, choose the *Select Chart* command. The chart is now marked with white squares. Switch on *Automatic* from *Border* in the *Format - Patterns* dialog box and click on the *Shadow* box.

In addition, you can also define the format of the border by changing the *Style, Color* and *Weight* settings. After you have confirmed the dialog box, EXCEL draws a border with a shadow around the chart. The markers disappear if you click outside the chart.

Now, from the *Chart* menu, activate the *Select Plot Area* command. This time, EXCEL marks a rectangle the size of the axes. This is the plot area. After you have switched on the *Automatic* button in *Border* from the *Format - Patterns* dialog box, your chart should look like this:

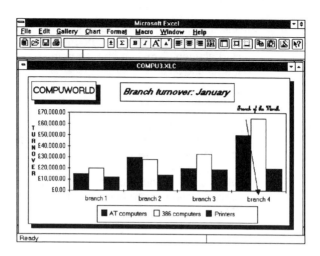

Exercise 28

If you have not yet incorporated the border described above into your COMPU3.XLC chart, do so now. Save the result using *File - Save*.

If you have a colour monitor, you can also colour in the chart and the plot area, and give it a pattern. On mono-chrome monitors, it is a good idea to stick to patterns on a white background.

Here, we also want to point out another problem: if you print a chart using a monochrome printer, EXCEL tries to replace the colours with various patterns. A coloured chart which may look excellent on the screen, will be disappointing when printed on paper.

In this case, we recommend saving the chart twice: once in colour and once in a format which the printer can represent accurately on paper.

To apply a colour or a pattern to part of a chart, select the required element and choose the *Patterns* com-mand from the *Format* menu.

In the *Area* list in the dialog box, you will find the pattern and the foreground and background colours for the selected element. You can choose from sixteen different patterns and colours.

Examples:

1   Yellow chart with blue diagonal pattern: choose the desired pattern, make the foreground blue and the background yellow.

2   Blue chart without pattern: choose blue for the foreground and background and do not choose a pattern.

Exercise 29

Try out several different colour combinations on the COMPU3.XLC chart. When you have finished, restore the original colours by loading the chart again.

Note:
You can also return to the original situation using the *Set Preferred* option from the *Gallery* menu. Use this command before you start the exercise. When you have finished, choose the *Gallery - Preferred* command to return to the original colour and pattern settings. However, the preference you have chosen only remains valid while you are working in EXCEL. The next time you start the program, it will be lost.

3.6.7   Dividing and formatting axes

The axes have a particularly strong influence on the shape of your chart. We can distinguish between the category axis (X axis) and the value axis (Y axis). EXCEL calculates the graduated scale for the axes using series values, gives the axes tick marks and where possible copies the tick labels from the worksheet upon which the chart is based.

The *Chart - Axes* and *Format - Scale* commands offer a wide range of formatting possibilities.

a) Displaying axes

The *Chart - Axes* command produces a dialog box containing a summary of the axes available in the active chart window. Here, we must make a distinction between the category and value axes for the main chart and those for an overlay chart, if applicable. Use the check boxes to define which axes are to be displayed in the chart. Do not change anything now, since we want to display both axes in our example.

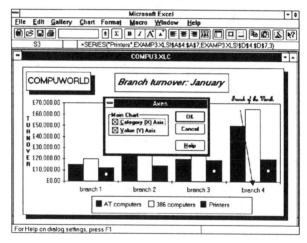

b) Scale

Using the *Scale* command from the *Format* menu, you can call up a dialog box in which you define the scale settings. Before you do this, select the axis whose scale settings you want to change. The options you see in the dialog box depend on the axis you select.

Value axis. Select the value axis in our example chart by clicking on it with the mouse and activate the *Format - Scale* command. You will see the following dialog box:

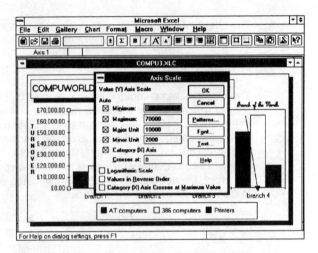

As you can see, EXCEL has chosen a range from a
minimum of 0 to a maximum of 70,000 for the value
axis. This range is subdivided into intervals of 10,000.
The highest value on our chart 65,000. The value axis is
therefore subdivided in an optimum way.

Exercise 30

Enter a *Maximum* of 120,000 and confirm the dialog box
using *OK*. Look at the difference in the chart, then restore the previous setting by checking the *Maximum*
box.

You can subdivide the primary graduated scale by activating *Minor Unit*. The way the minor tick marks are displayed is determined using *Format - Patterns*.

If you activate the *Values in Reverse Order* box from the
Scale command, the chart is displayed as a mirror
image. The category axis with the zero values is now at
the top. The intersection of the value and category axes
is set as standard at 0. Moving this intersection produces some interesting application possibilities.

Exercise 31

Imagine the boss of COMPUWORLD has fixed a monthly turnover target of £25,000 for each product group. Enter this value at *Category (X) Axis Crosses at.*

If you now look at the chart in the next illustration, you will see, above the category axis, where the target turnover has been achieved and where it has not been achieved.

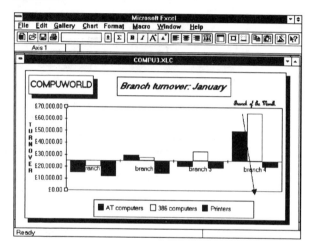

Now restore the original chart.

Note:
This type of change moves attached text with it. Unattached text remains where it is, as can be seen from the arrow. Any required adaptations can be made manually.

Category axis. After you have selected the category axis, use the *Format - Scale* command to call up the following dialog box to set the graduated scale of this axis:

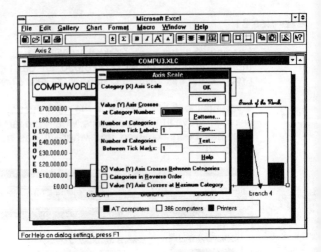

- At the top, define the point of intersection with the value axis. If you type a 3 in the *Value (Y) Axis Crosses at Category Number*, EXCEL places the value axis between categories 2 and 3. This is not a good idea for our example because the tick labels on the value axis will then be overlaid on the bars of category 2.

- If you set the *Number of Categories Between Tick Labels* at 2, a tick label is only assigned to every other category. This can be useful for narrow categories or long tick labels.

- Using *Number of Categories Between Tick Marks*, you can determine the category after which tick marks are to be displayed. If we enter the value 2 in our example, we only see a tick mark between categories 2 and 3.

- The *Value (Y) Axis Crosses Between Categories* box is checked as standard. This setting ensures that the value axis does not run through the middle of the category defined in the first box.

- If you switch on *Categories in Reverse Order*, the categories are displayed from right to left.

- *Value (Y) Axis Crosses at Maximum Category* places the value axis beside the last category with the highest number.

Exercise 32

Try out these options, then restore the original chart when you have finished.

c) Formatting axes

Before you can format an axis, you must first select it. The command needed to format the axes can be found in the *Format* menu. You can switch directly from the dialog box of one command to that of the three others. The *Format - Patterns* dialog box now looks like this:

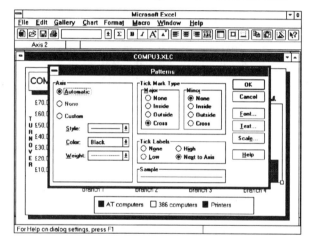

The style, colour and weight of the axis are specified at *Axis.* You will already be familiar with this from *Border. Tick Mark Type* is used to determine whether the major or minor tick marks have to be displayed. If so, you can also determine whether the tick marks are to be placed inside, outside or across the axis line. Similarly, you can determine the location of the tick labels.

If you switch to the *Font* dialog box, you can set the text format of the tick labels. You can choose from the options described in section 3.6.2.

Exercise 33

1   In chart COMPU3.XLC choose type style MS Sans
    Serif, size 8, regular, blue for the tick labels on the
    value axis.

2   In chart COMPU3.XLC choose type style MS Sans
    Serif, size 10, bold, blue for the tick labels on the ca-
    tegory axis.

3   Save the result using *File - Save.*

3.6.8   Gridlines

On a chart with many categories, optional lines extending from the tick marks on an axis across the entire
chart can make the chart much easier to handle. These
so-called **gridlines** are generated using the *Gridlines*
command from the *Chart* menu.

Using the dialog box, you can switch on major and
minor gridlines for both the category and value axes. In
the *Format - Patterns* dialog box, you can define the format of the gridlines. The major and minor unit settings
for the category and value axes determine the weight of
the gridline.

Exercise 34

1   Overlay a major grid on the value and category axes
    in the COMPU3.XLC chart.

2   Save the result using *File - Save.*

Your chart should now look like this:

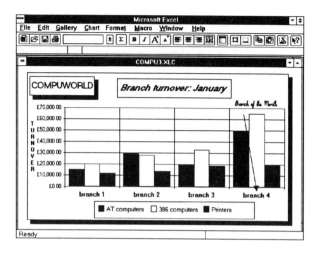

Our example chart is now complete. Finally, just one piece of advice. Do not make your charts too full and do not use too many format options. You do not have to use every available choice. Often, limited use of the format options produces the best results. In contrast, too many fonts, styles, patterns and weights can confuse rather than simplify the presentation.

3.7 Questions and answers

Question 3-1: Pie chart

COMPUWORLDS's management wants a summary of the turnover achieved by the four branches in January, in the form of a pie chart showing percentages. The names of the branches must be shown in the pie segments. The chart should have a frame and then be printed.

Answer

1 From worksheet EXAMP3.XLS, select the column containing the branch turnover.

2 Create a new chart using *File - New*.

3 From the *Gallery - Pie* dialog box, choose the sixth format.

4 Add the names of the branches to the chart in the form of unattached text.

5 Place a border around the chart.

6 Print out the result.

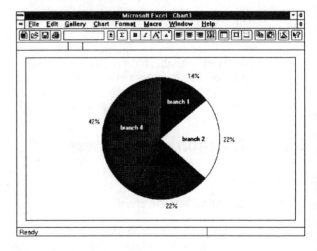

Question 3-2: Comparison of depreciation methods

In question 2-5, you created worksheet DE-PREC.XLS to compare three different depreciation methods. The development of the depreciation amounts for a purchase price of £80,000, service life of 30 years and a residual value of £500 must now be displayed as a line chart. The title of the print out is 'Depreciation Amounts Using Various Depreciation Methods'. The name of the relevant depreciation method is given beside each curve: retrogressive depreciation, linear depreciation and digital depreciation. An arrow shows where retrogressive depreciation switches over to linear depreciation. The category axis has the caption 'Service Life'. The chart is to be printed on one entire page.

Answer

1   Load the DEPREC.XLS worksheet, enter the values in the question and mark the columns with the depreciation amounts.

2   Create a new chart using *File - New*.

3   Click on *OK* (First Data Series).

4   In the *Gallery - Line* dialog box, choose the fourth format.

5   Add the chart title.

6   Add the names for the curves as unattached text.

7   Add borders, shadows and select *Automatic* in the *Area* part of the *Patterns* dialog box.

8   Add the arrow.

9 Select *Use Full Page* in the *Page Setup* dialog box.

10 Look at the sample print.

11 Print out the chart.

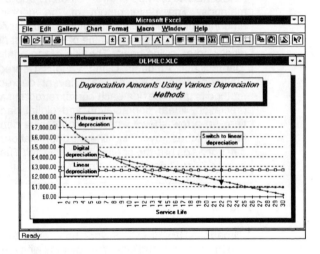

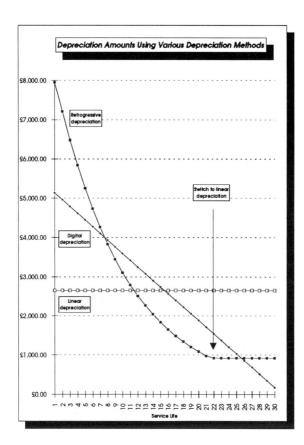

DEPREC.XLC

Depreciation Amounts Using Various Depreciation Methods

Page 1

4   Databases

4.1   Creating a database

4.1.1   Terminology

In addition to worksheets and charts, EXCEL also has a third function - databases. These can be used to store, change, arrange, search and analyse data using various criteria.

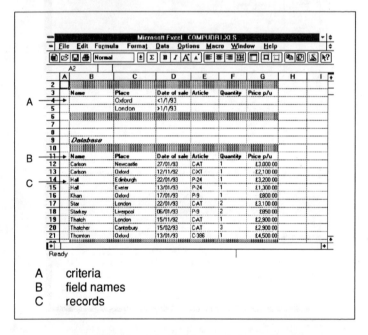

A   criteria
B   field names
C   records

A **database** is a collection of data, the elements of which can be addressed in different ways. EXCEL's definition of a database is a **range within a worksheet to which the name 'database' is assigned.** This database range is a rectangular area of cells in a worksheet. The rows in this range are used to enter records.

A **record** contains the data saved via an object. A customer record can thus contain the name of the customer, his/her address, turnover, etc.. All records in one database have the same structure and within a record, the data are grouped into fields.

The top row of the database range is intended for the **field names.** Using field names, individual fields within a record can be addressed.

To request particular records, **search criteria** can be given in a **criterion range**.

Using **comparison criteria**, the user specifies a value with which particular fields in the database range are compared in order to request the required data. It is therefore possible to request all records with the postcode OX1 1AA or with a turnover > £2000.

When using **computed criteria**, the search criterion is only generated after a calculation using particular fields in a record. For example, the payment deadline is exceeded if invoice date + payment deadline > current date.

Using search criteria, selected records can be placed in a reserved section of the worksheet, known as the **extract range.**

4.1.2   Preparing a database

Before you start creating a database it is worth giving some serious thought to its structure. We want to illustrate this using an example:

The manager of COMPUWORLD's branch 1 wants to be able to select particular groups of customers from an EXCEL worksheet, for advertising purposes.

In this case, a record must be made for every sale - we

must therefore decide which fields have to be included in the record. For example, we can think of a record consisting of the name of the customer, the address, the date of sale, a description of the product bought, the quantity and price.

In this type of record division, it is possible to establish who bought what, where, when and in what quantity. It is also possible to check whether a particular customer bought a particular product before or after a certain date.

The search criteria can be linked with logical AND and logical OR. For example, it is possible to request all customers who bought a printer before a certain date (AND link). It is also possible to select all customers who have bought either a printer or a plotter (OR link). We can also combine AND and OR links, for example to request all customers in locations A and B who have bought a printer.

4.1.3   Creating a database

We are now going to create the database described above. Let's start by reserving the required database range.

A worksheet can only contain one database range with the name 'Database'. However, it is possible to set up several database ranges in a worksheet but they must have different names. But the name 'Database' must always be assigned first to the range to be edited.

It is not absolutely necessary to set up the database range in full. The final number of records will probably not be known beforehand. Simply leave a few rows free at the end of the database range. It is a good idea to mark the end of the database range by shading it.

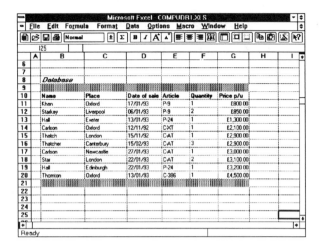

For our example, ten records will be sufficient.

Proceed as follows:

1 Type the field names in the first row: name, place, date of sale, article, quantity, price per unit. This division automatically applies to all records.

2 Set the column width and format the cells.

3 Copy the records into the cells under the field names.

4 Select the range from the row with the field names to the row with the shadow format. Both rows belong to the range to be selected.

5 Choose the *Set Database* command from the *Data* menu. The name 'Database' is now assigned to the selected range.

The database is ready. Save the result under the name COMPUDB1.XLS.

4.2   Editing a database

4.2.1   Adding records

Entering data into a database is similar to entering data in a table.

But what happens if records have to be added to an existing database range? Select the row under the database range and add one or more empty rows using the *Insert* command from the *Edit* menu. The end of the database range is automatically moved downwards and you can now add the new records.

Similarly, you can include new fields by adding columns in the database range.

4.2.2   Changing records

We will only deal with changing records here for the sake of completeness. As when changing a table, select the relevant cell and edit the cell contents in the formula bar. Confirm the changes using Enter or by clicking on the enter box.

4.2.3   Deleting records

You must first find the record you want to delete. Using the knowledge we have acquired so far, we have no choice but to search systematically through the database range, row by row. This is extremely laborious if the database files are very large. When the record has been found it can be deleted using the *Delete* command from the *Edit* menu (*Entire Row*).

However, we are not going to discuss these methods of inserting and deleting records any further at this point, since section 4.4 will show you a much easier way of editing a database.

4.2.4 Sorting records

It is not essential to enter the records in a particular order. EXCEL is capable of a wide range of sorting functions.

We are now going to sort our database by customer name. First select the range to be sorted. If you have chosen the same division as in the previous example, that will be range B11:G20. Do not select the first row, with the field names, or the last row, with the shadow format, since these do not have to be sorted.

Then define the sort criteria. This is done in the dialog box which appears on the screen when you use the *Data - Sort* command:

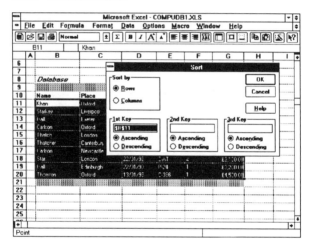

If the dialog box is overlaid on an important part of the database range, you can move it to one side by clicking on the title bar and dragging the window.

At the top of the dialog box, you can define whether sorting is to take place by row or by column. We shall leave our database at the standard *Rows* setting.

At the bottom, you can specify a maximum of three sort keys, and you can set whether each key is to be sorted in ascending or descending order.

Since we want to sort in ascending order by one key ('Name'), we must specify the reference in the 'Name' column in the box for key 1, in this case $B$11. It is very simple to enter information in the key boxes using the mouse:

1 Position the *Sort* dialog box so that the first record is visible.

2 In the dialog box, click in the relevant key box.

3 In the first record of the database range, click on the field which is to serve as the sort key.

After confirming with *OK*, the database range is sorted.

Exercise 35

The database must be sorted in ascending order by article, in ascending order by customer name within the articles and in descending order by date of sale within this group. Sort correspondingly.

	B	C	D	E	F	G	H	I
8	*Database*							
9								
10	**Name**	**Place**	**Date of sale**	**Article**	**Quantity**	**Price p/u**		
11	Thornton	Oxford	13/01/93	C-386	1	£4,500.00		
12	Carlson	Newcastle	27/01/93	C-AT	1	£3,000.00		
13	Star	London	22/01/93	C-AT	2	£3,100.00		
14	Thatch	London	15/11/92	C-AT	1	£2,900.00		
15	Thatcher	Canterbury	15/02/93	C-AT	3	£2,900.00		
16	Carlson	Oxford	12/11/92	C-XT	1	£2,100.00		
17	Hall	Edinburgh	22/01/93	P-24	1	£3,200.00		
18	Hall	Exeter	13/01/93	P-24	1	£1,300.00		
19	Khan	Oxford	17/01/93	P-9	1	£800.00		
20	Starkey	Liverpool	06/01/93	P-9	2	£950.00		

As you can see, the keys with a higher number are sub-groups of the keys with a lower number.

If you want to sort by more than three keys, you must sort more frequently. The last sorting process always defines the main order.

When you sort *per column*, you also select the field names. If you now choose the field names as the sort key, the result is usually a fairly meaningless alphabetical arrangement per column name.

With a bit of skill, it is possible to arrange the columns differently. Insert an empty record as the first row of the database range and in every field type the desired column number. If you sort according to these numbers, you will achieve the required column order.

Sorting method:

1 Select the range to be sorted.

2 Choose the *Sort* command from the *Data* menu.

3 Specify the sort keys or choose them with the mouse.

4 Start the sorting process by clicking on the *OK* button.

Now sort the database in ascending order by name.

4.3 Finding records

4.3.1 Defining the criterion range

When you are searching for records you do not need to go through an entire database. EXCEL can address individual records for a particular purpose. In our example, we can use this function to establish quickly which customers have bought an AT computer but no printer in the past six months.

For this purpose, the database range has to be extended by a **criterion range** which determines how, and using which fields, the records are searched. It is a good idea to place this criterion range immediately to the left, right, above or below the database range, since it is more accessible this way. You will now also understand why we have not yet used the first eight rows of the worksheet.

The criterion range consists of a minimum of two rows and one column. The first row contains the **criterion names** and the row(s) under it the criteria themselves.

In our example, we want to be able to use all the fields in the record as search criteria.

1   Copy all the field names in row 10 (B10:G10) from the database range to row 3 using the *Copy* and *Paste* commands from the *Edit* menu. You have now defined the criterion names.

2   Now select the range B3:G4 as the criterion range, in this case the row with the field names (criterion names) and the empty row below it.

3   Choose the *Set Criteria* command from the *Data* menu.

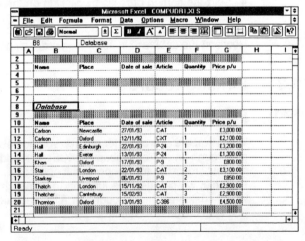

The criterion range is now defined. You are not obliged to include all field names as criterion names. Only use the criteria you really need.

4.3.2 Types of criteria and criterion names

When we discussed terminology at the beginning of this chapter, we referred to the difference between comparison criteria and computed criteria.

Comparison criteria are texts or values used as comparison arguments when choosing records. The field names from the database range are usually used as criterion names. These are copied to the criterion range, which we also did in our previous example.

Computed criteria relate the comparison arguments in calculations to values from the database and/or values outside the database range. It is a good idea to use names which explain the computed find criteria.

4.3.3 Finding values

Finding records using comparison criteria

In our example, we want to find all customers who live in London.

1 Select cell C4 in the criterion range.

2 Type 'London'.

3 Choose the *Find* command from the *Data* menu.

EXCEL then searches the database range and marks the first row which satisfies the find criterion. In our example, this is row 16.

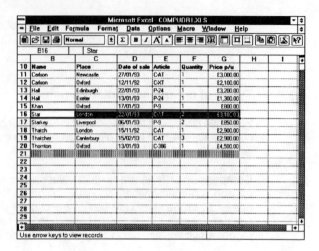

Use the cursor keys or click on the scroll arrow to find the next record which satisfies the criteria. The new pattern in the scroll bars indicates that find mode is active. To leave search mode:

■ choosing the *Exit Find* command from the *Data* menu
■ pressing Esc
■ clicking outside the database range.

If no records are found, EXCEL leaves the search mode by giving the message 'Could not find matching data.'

Method:

1 Click on the relevant cell in the criterion range.

2 Specify the find criterion.

3 Choose the *Find* command from the *Data* menu.

4 Look at the records found in the database range.

5 Exit find mode.

Find records using wildcard characters and comparison operators as search criteria

When you are using text as a find criterion, it is also possible to find parts of a text.

If we specify the letter T for 'Name' in the criterion range, EXCEL searches for all names with this initial letter. If we specify 'Thatch' as the search criterion, we will find not only Mr Thatch, but also Mr Thatcher. To find only customers with the name Thatch, we must specify the following: ="=Thatch".

Using the wildcard characters * and ?, with which you are no doubt already familiar from using DOS, you can specify placeholders for a random series of characters or for individual characters. If you specify 'P*' in the 'Article' criterion field, you can find all the printers. The criterion 'C-?T' finds all XT and AT computers.

Further possibilities for defining subseries can be achieved by using comparison operators. To obtain a summary of all sales before 1 January 1993, we would type the criterion '<1/1/93' in the 'Date of sale' criterion field. If we typed '>2000' in the 'Price p/u' field, we could request all sales above £2,000.

Exercise 36

Try out the possibilities described above on worksheet COMPUDB1.XLS.

Combining search criteria

It is also possible to search for records using several search criteria. This is necessary, for example, if you are searching for all customers in Oxford who have bought a computer. You would then type 'Oxford' in the 'Place' criterion field and 'C' in 'Article'. If you are looking for all customers who bought a printer before 10

January 1993, the 'Date of sale' criterion would be
'<10/1/93' and 'Article' would be 'P'.

These combinations are **AND links**. These can be specified in one row. For **OR links** you must use several
rows. Imagine you are looking for customers in Oxford
who bought an article before 1 January 1993 and customers in London who bought an article after 1 January
1993.

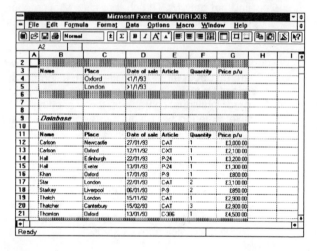

You need a criterion range of two rows.

1 Select the range B3:G5.

2 Choose the *Set Criteria* command from the *Data*
   menu.

3 In the criterion fields, type:

Place   Date of Sale

Oxford <1/1/93

London >1/1/93

Exercise 37

Try out this example.

Finding records using computed criteria

Computed criteria use formulas related to fields in the database. Their results are the logical values TRUE or FALSE.

Example:
We are looking for all records of sales of more than £4,500. We cannot find this value in our database. But it is still possible to calculate it by multiplying the quantity and price fields. We can do this by extending the criterion range with a field called 'Total'. In the new 'Total' field, we enter the formula '=G11*F11>4500'.

In this type of formula you can also address cells outside the database range. However, you should then use absolute references.

A record counts as having been found when testing the calculated fields against the formula produces TRUE or not equal to zero. In all other cases, a record is passed over.

4.4   Extracting records

It is also possible to copy all the records found from the database to another section of the worksheet, the **extract range**, or to another file. This is called **extracting.** The extract range is exactly the same as the criterion range in terms of structure, but it has a different function. The extract range must therefore be outside the database range.

This is how to copy records from the database to the extract range:

1   Specify search criteria in the criterion range.

2   Copy the required field names to the first row of the extract range.

3   Define the extract range by selecting the field names and choosing the *Set Extract* command from the *Data* menu.

4   Choose the *Extract* command from the *Data* menu.

5   Decide whether or not only unique records are to be extracted.

EXCEL copies the records found to the extract range. The following example shows a request for a list of all customers who have bought more than one item of an article.

Criterion range					
Name	Place	Date of sale	Article	Quantity	Price p/u
				>1	

Database					
Name	Place	Date of sale	Article	Quantity	Price p/u
Carlson	Newcastle	27/01/93	C-AT	1	£3,000.00
Carlson	Oxford	12/11/92	C-XT	1	£2,100.00
Hall	Edinburgh	22/01/93	P-24	1	£3,200.00
Hall	Exeter	13/01/93	P-24	1	£1,300.00
Khan	Oxford	17/01/93	P-9	1	£800.00
Star	London	22/01/93	C-AT	2	£3,100.00
Starkey	Liverpool	06/01/93	P-9	2	£850.00
Thatch	London	15/11/92	C-AT	1	£2,900.00
Thatcher	Canterbury	15/02/93	C-AT	3	£2,900.00
Thornton	Oxford	13/01/93	C-386	1	£4,500.00

Extract range			
Name	Place	Article	Quantity
Star	London	C-AT	2
Starkey	Liverpool	P-9	2
Thatcher	Canterbury	C-AT	3

If we select only the row with the field names as the extract range, all the records found will be copied into the rows below. However, it is also possible to restrict the extract range to a particular number of records. For example, to extract five of the customers who satisfy particular criteria, select another five rows in addition to the row with the field names. EXCEL then extracts five records and stops searching.

If you want to copy records to another worksheet, set up a criterion range in the other worksheet, with search criteria and an extract range. Using the *Formula - Define Name* command, assign the name *'Database'*. Give the worksheet from which the records are to be extracted as an external reference, e.g. COMPUDB1.XLS!Database.

4.5   Using a data form

EXCEL offers yet another way of performing the operations described above, in the shape of what is known
as a data form. Using a data form, you can view,
change or erase records. The data form operates inde-
pendently of the editing commands in the *Data* menu
and without a criterion range. You can also enter,
search or copy data using the data form.

4.5.1   Using the standard data form

Using the *Form* command from the *Data* menu, request
the standard data form for the relevant worksheet. Here
you can browse through your database record by record.

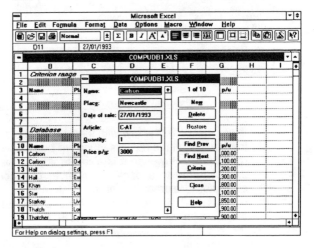

You can move the data form by clicking on the title bar,
holding down the left mouse button and dragging the
data form across the screen.

On the left, you will see the fields for the current record
from the database. The text boxes with the data are
situated after the field names. You can change the data

in these boxes. Computed fields are displayed without a text box to indicate that you cannot edit them in the data form.

In the top right-hand corner of the data form you will see what is known as the **position indicator**, which indicates which record is displayed. Under it is a series of buttons which are used to start the various functions.

There is a scroll bar between the text boxes and the buttons. You can use this to browse through the database. The position of the scroll button on the bar gives the approximate location of the record in the database.

4.5.2 Editing records in the data form

In the data form, you can only edit records of no more than fourteen fields. The data form is requested using the *Data - Form* command and exited using the *Close* button. If you want to undo the changes you have made, click on the *Restore* button. Enter is used to confirm all changes. EXCEL then shows the next record.

The *New* button is used to add records. If you click on it, the scroll button automatically jumps to the end of the scroll bar and the position indicator shows 'New Record'. The text boxes are now empty. Using the mouse, you can select the box where you want to enter data. It is also possible to choose the individual fields using key combination Alt and the underlined letter in the relevant field name. After entering, use Enter to add the record to the database.

To erase the record from the data form, click on the *Delete* button. As a safety measure, EXCEL requests confirmation, because it is not possible to retrieve a record which has been erased in this way using the *Restore* option.

To browse the database for particular records, first specify the search criteria. This is done using the *Criteria* button.

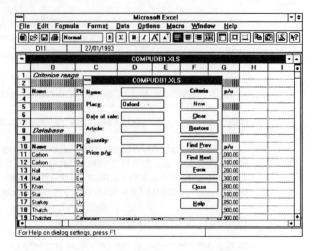

The text 'Criteria' appears on the top right of the data
form. Some of the buttons now have a different name.
The field names, with empty text boxes, appear on the
left of the data form. As discussed earlier, here you can
specify search criteria. However, it is not possible to use
computed search criteria or OR links in the data form.

After entering the search criteria, you can browse your
database forwards or backwards using the *Find Next*
and *Find Prev* buttons. Use the *Form* button to stop the
search. The data form then returns to its usual format.
To exit the data form, click on the *Close* button. The
data form disappears from the screen.

4.5.3   Creating a data form

You can create a data form yourself and save it with the
corresponding database. You can define the data form
in a range of the worksheet to which you assign the
name 'Data_Form'. A custom data form has the same
parts as a standard data form, but you yourself can
define the position of the boxes in the left-hand section
of the data form. The buttons and the scroll bar remain
the same.

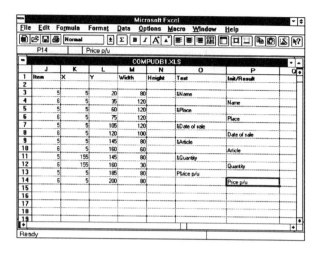

The first row of the 'Data_Form' range (J2:P14) must be empty. We will use seven cells per row to define a component of the data form:

1 **Item**:
   5   static text
   6   text box

2 **X:** the horizontal position of the component, with respect to the top left-hand corner of the data form.

3 **Y:** the vertical position of the component, with respect to the top left-hand corner of the data form.

4 **Width:** the width of the component.

5 **Height:** the height of the component.

6 **Text:** the statistical text (e.g. the field name). The character after & is underlined.

7 **Init/Result:** contains the relevant field names from the database for type 6.

A little calculation is required to define the coordinates

of a component. For vertical positions you have to use
1/12 of the height of a character in the chosen type style
and, for horizontal positions 1/8 of the width. The correct position and dimensions of a component are
defined by specifying its values and looking at the result. The 'Height' column is empty since the height of
the field is automatically adjusted to accomodate the
font.

Before you can use the customised data form, you must
assign the name 'Data_Form' to the range where you
have defined this custom data form.

Exercise 38

1   Load worksheet COMPUDB1.XLS and copy the data
    for the 'Data_Form' from the previous illustration.

2   Name this range 'Data_Form'.

3   Save the worksheet.

4   Choose the *Data - Form* command. The data form
    should now look like this:

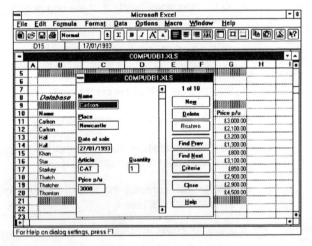

4.6   Using database functions

In Chapter 2 we discussed using worksheet functions.
EXCEL has twelve special functions designed for ana-
lysing a database. The names of all these functions
begin with **DB** for database.

After the name of the functions, three arguments appear in parentheses. The syntax is therefore:

DBfunction(database,field,criteria)

The *database* argument refers to the database range.
This reference can be specified as **cell range** (e.g.
B10:G20) or as **range name**. In our COMPUDB1.XLS
worksheet, the database range B10:G20 was automatically given the name 'Database' after the *Data - Set Database* command. This name can be used as the argument in a database function.

The *field* argument defines which field in the database
is used for the calculation. The field name in the first column of the database is used as a field reference. It is
also possible to replace this name by the corresponding
column number, i.e. 1 for 'Name', 2 for 'Place', etc..

The *criteria* argument is the reference to the database
criterion range, and can be specified as a field reference (B3:G4) or as a range name. In our example, the
criterion range was automatically given the name 'Criteria' after the *Data - Set Criteria* command. The database functions accept this name for the *criteria* argument.

We are now going to apply a few database functions in
the COMPUDB1.XLS worksheet. You can specify them
in cell B6.

DCOUNT(database,"quantity",criteria)
If you specify 2 in the criterion range under *Quantity*,
this function counts how many of the *Quantity* fields
contain a number and in how many of them the value 2

appears. In our example, the function produces the value 2.

DCOUNT(database,"name",criteria)
The function now produces the value 0, because none of the *Name* fields contain a number. (Remove the value 2 from the criterion range.)

DCOUNTA(database,"name",criteria)
This function counts the *Name* fields which satisfy the search criteria. The result is 10.

DMAX(database,"price p/u",criteria)
The function establishes which *Price p/u* fields satisfy the criteria and searches through them for the field with the highest value. If we specify '<1/1/93' in the criterion range for *Date of sale,* this function produces 2900. If we specify '>1/1/93' the result is 4500.

DMIN(database,"price p/u",criteria)
In contrast to DMAX, this function looks for the lowest value, thus for date of sale '<1/1/93' the value 2100 and for date of sale '>1/1/93' the value 800.

DSUM(database,"quantity",criteria)
If we specify '<1/1/93' in the criterion range for *Date of sale,* and 'London' for *Place,* this function produces the quantities sold before 1 January 1993 in London, in this case therefore 1.

DAVERAGE(database,"price p/u",criteria)
This function produces the average of all the values in the *Price p/u* field which satisfy the criteria.

DPRODUCT(database,field,criteria)
This function multiplies together the values in the *field* field which satisfy the criteria.

The other functions are for the statistical analysis of a database. You can request information on the use of these functions at any time by calling up the EXCEL help system, using F1.

Exercise 39

Try out the database functions on worksheet COM-PUDB1.XLS.

4.7   Questions and answers

Branch 2 of COMPUWORLD uses an EXCEL database. The illustration below shows a section of it.

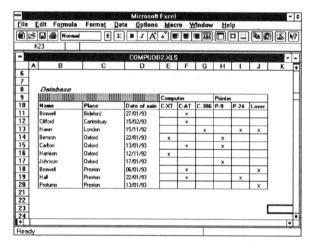

Question 4-1
Create a new worksheet and copy this database into it. Save the worksheet under the name COMPUDB2.XLS.

Question 4-2
Sort the database in ascending order according to customer name and, within customer name, per date of sale.

Question 4-3
a) Search the database for customers in Oxford who have bought an XT computer.
b) Search for customers who have bought a laser printer.

Question 4-4

a) Request all customers in Oxford who have bought an AT computer and all customers in Preston who have bought a laser printer.

b) Request all customers in Oxford and Preston who bought a computer or a printer before 7 January 1993.

Answer to question 4-1

Copy the data and format for the worksheet from the illustration. Remember to define the database range (B10:J20).

Answer to question 4-2

Select the database range B11:J20. Choose the *Sort* command from the *Data* menu and specify the sort keys by clicking on the relevant fields in the first row of the database.

Answer to question 4-3

Set up the criterion range B2:J3. This consists of a row with field names and an empty row.

a) Specify 'Oxford' for the *Place* find criteria and 'x' for *C-XT*. Define the range B2:J3 as the criterion range using the *Set Criteria* command from the *Data* menu. Then start the search process using *Data - Find*.

b) Clear the previous find criteria, state 'x' for *Laser* and start the search process again as described earlier.

Answer to question 4-4

To extract, you will need an extract range. Copy the two rows with the column titles and field names for the database to row 27 and define the range B27:J37 as the extract range, using the *Data - Set Extract* command. To answer this question you must extend the criterion range by one row. To do this, select the range B2:J4 and choose the *Data - Set Criteria* command.

a) Specify the following find criteria: in the first row 'Oxford' for *Place* and 'x' for *C-AT*, in the second row 'Preston' for *Place* and 'x' for *Laser*. Before you start the find process, select the row with the field names for the extract range and choose the *Data - Set Ex-*

tract command, to define the extract range.

b) Specify the following search criteria: in the first row 'Oxford' for *Place* and '<7/1/93' for *Date of sale*, and in the second row 'Preston' for *Place* and '<7/1/93' for *Date of sale*. Once you have defined the extract range again, you can start the search process. The following illustration shows the result:

Criterion range

Name	Place	Date of sale	C-XT	C-AT	C-386	P-9	P-24	Laser
	Oxford	<7/1/93						
	Preston	<7/1/93						

Database

| Name | Place | Date of sale | Computer | | | Printer | | |
			C-XT	C-AT	C-386	P-9	P-24	Laser
Benson	Oxford	22/01/93	x			x		
Boswell	Preston	06/01/93		x				x
Boswell	Bideford	27/01/93		x				
Carlton	Oxford	13/01/93		x		x		
Clifford	Canterbury	15/02/93		x				
Hall	Preston	22/01/93		x			x	
Harrison	Oxford	12/11/92	x					
Hawn	London	15/11/92			x		x	x
Johnson	Oxford	17/01/93				x		
Profumo	Preston	13/01/93						x

Extract range

| Name | Place | Date of sale | Computer | | | Printer | | |
			C-XT	C-AT	C-386	P-9	P-24	Laser
Boswell	Preston	06/01/93		x				x
Harrison	Oxford	12/11/92	x					

5   Macros

5.1   Basic knowledge for working with macros

A macro is a series of recorded commands which can
be played back later. Commands refer to all operations
performed using the keyboard and the mouse. A macro
is always given a name and a keyboard combination.
This is how the macro is started. Using macros has certain advantages, such as:

- **Faster operation.** A long series of commands can
  be performed using one key combination.
- **Automation of regular activities.** Instead of performing a series of commands time and again, you can
  record them as a macro.
- **Simplification of complex worksheets.** By developing customised functions, you can display complex, difficult formulas much more clearly.
- **More user-friendly operation.** By developing specific menus and dialog boxes for a worksheet using
  EXCEL's macrolanguage, it is possible to simplify
  worksheet operations to the extent that a beginner
  can use the worksheets with relatively little knowledge of the program.
- **Data exchange possibilities with other Windows
  applications.** Using macros, it is possible to exchange data with other programs and to start other
  programs.

EXCEL has a highly sophisticated macrolanguage. In
contrast to macros in other programs, EXCEL macros
are saved separately from the worksheet in a specific
file, known as the **macro sheet**.
This means that a macro can be used in several worksheets. As with worksheets and charts, the file name of
a macro sheet consists of a name of a maximum of
eight characters and the extension .XLM (e.g.

MACRO1.XLM). A macro sheet can contain any number of macros. EXCEL has two types of macros - command macros and function macros or *custom functions*.

A **command macro** performs a series of actions. Accordingly, it is possible to make new commands using menu options, functions and special macro functions, for example to give selected cells a border or to print a worksheet with particular headers and footers.

A **custom function** is a function developed by the user, which produces a value. Arguments (entered values) must therefore be transferred to a custom function. For example, a custom function could be developed which automatically calculates the price including VAT of gross prices.

There are various ways of making a command macro. You can enter the macro row by row in the macro sheet. However, it is quicker to record a macro using the EXCEL **macro recorder**. This recording can still be manually edited afterwards.

In contrast, a function macro is always entered manually.

5.2   How to make a macro

When you want to make a macro:

1 Define the task of the macro
As in the case of programming using a programming language, it is a good idea when writing a macro to analyse and consider seriously the tasks the macro is to perform. What does the macro have to do? Does it have to perform a series of complex commands or do you want to control the macro's processes with input? Do worksheets or charts have to be displayed on the screen or printed? How do you iron out mistakes?

2   Define the structure of the macro
Sketch the course of the macro. What are the steps it has to perform, and in what order? You can use a flow chart or a structogram for this sketch. See if you can work with modules, which means using various small macros linked together by a control macro.

3   Make the macro
When you have finished this preparation, you can make the macro. First, open a new macro sheet. Then, step by step, type the commands into the sheet. If you are making a command macro, you can also use the macro recorder for recording. In this case, remember to switch the recorder off after the last operation.

Then, give the macro a name. For a command macro, you can choose not just a name, but also a key combination. This can be an upper or lower case letter, combined with the Ctrl key. The macro can be started using this key combination. You cannot specify key combinations for function macros.

4   Test the macro
To be sure that the macro does actually work perfectly, it is a good idea to test it thoroughly. Here, it is very useful to be able to run the macro step by step.

5   Document the macro
We recommend extensively documenting the macro so that it can be processed at a later date. The macro sheet offers adequate room for this. You can also make cell notes.

5.3   Command macros

5.3.1   Creating a macro

We shall use a simple example as our first exercise.

Task. We want to make a macro which puts a border

around previously selected cells. Furthermore, we want to separate adjacent cells of columns within the range by a line.

Text analysis and structure. The selection of cells must not form part of the macro, otherwise the same range will always be given a border. The macro must perform the following steps:

1 Choose the *Format - Border* command.

2 Click on the *Outline* box in the *Format - Border* dialog box.

3 Click on the *Left* box in the *Format - Border* dialog box.

4 Click on the *OK* button.

Record the macro. In the *Macro* menu, you will see two commands which can be used to start recording. If you choose *Record,* EXCEL opens a new macro sheet. If a macro sheet is already loaded, EXCEL writes the macro in the first free column of this sheet.

The other command is *Start Recorder.* This is used to write a macro in particular cells of an existing macro sheet.

We shall now choose the first command and activate *Macro - Record.* In the dialog box which will now appear on the screen, EXCEL suggests 'Record1' as a name for the macro, and key combination Ctrl with 'a'. Change the name to 'Border' and the key combination letter to 'b'. EXCEL also distinguishes between upper and lower case letters. If you specify a lower case letter, you have to start the macro using Ctrl and the relevant letter, e.g. Ctrl-A. If you specify an upper case letter, you must start the macro using Shift-Ctrl and the relevant letter, e.g. Shift-Ctrl-A.

You can now start recording. You will see the message

'Recording' at the bottom of the screen. Choose the *Format - Border* command and the *Outline* and *Left* boxes in the relevant dialog box. Confirm the dialog box with *OK* and end recording using *Macro - Stop Recorder*.

Macro sheet. If you now open the *Window* menu, you will see that EXCEL has automatically opened a new window with the name 'Macro1'. This is a macro sheet with the macro which has just been recorded. Switch to this window by clicking on its name. In terms of basic structure, the macro sheet looks like a worksheet. However, the columns are a little wider.

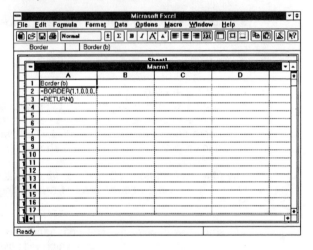

Macro structure. The macro recorder has written the macro in the first column row by row. The name you have specified for the macro is shown at the top. Macro formulas always start with an equal sign (=), just like worksheet formulas. The macro ends with the formula =RETURN(). Every macro has the following basic structure:

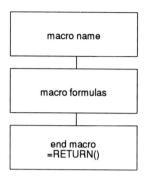

The BORDER macro function has the same setting possibilities as the *Border* command from the *Format* menu. If a setting is chosen, this is either 'TRUE' (1) or 'FALSE'. (0)

Test the macro. The macro is ready for use straight away. Switch to a worksheet window, e.g. 'Sheet1'. Select the range B2:D6 and press Ctrl-B. The selected range is given a border. Within the range, columns B, C and D are separated by a line. Since we did not include the range selection in the macro, we can apply this to any selected range. Give this a try. You can see the result better if you switch off the gridlines using *Options - Display*.

Documentation. Always document your macros. The name of the macro, comments and notes are particularly useful for documenting. When you name the macro make sure, if possible, that its operation is clear from the name. In our example, 'Border_Outline' would have been more apt. Comments are written in the column next to the macro formulas, where you can explain individual formulas. It is also important to name the key combination. You must not use any equal signs (=) because these are used to introduce formulas. It is better to use cell notes for extensive explanations. To do this, choose the *Formula - Note* command.

To distinguish comments and explanations clearly from the macro formulas, you can use the usual format possibilities. An example is given in the following illustration:

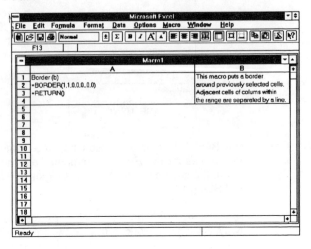

Exercise 40

Our macro sheet is still loaded. Switch to this sheet using the *Window* menu. If part of the window is visible, you can also activate it by clicking on it. Copy the comments and the format from the illustration.

Exercise 41

We are now going to continue with a revision exercise. To give worksheets a uniform format, we can record a macro to perform the following tasks:

1 Switch off the gridlines (*Options* menu - *Display*).

2 Switch off the display of zero values (*Options* menu - *Display*).

3 Choose the colour blue for the gridlines and the row and column headings (*Options* menu - *Display* - *Gridline & Heading Color*).

4 Make the window full-screen size (maximize button).

5 Save the worksheet.

Give this macro the name 'Format' (Ctrl-F).

Note:
Record the macro in the range A6:A10 in the existing macro sheet. Use the command 'Record' from the *Macro* menu. Proceed as follows:

1 Select cell A6.

2 Choose the *Set Recorder* command from the *Macro* menu.
3 Switch to your worksheet, e.g. to 'Sheet1'.

4 Choose the *Record* command from the Macro menu.

4 Apply the format described above.

6 Choose the *Stop Recorder* command from the Macro menu.

The result looks like this:

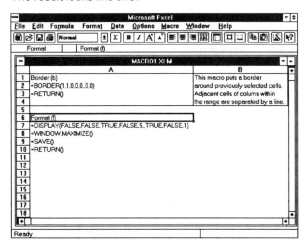

You can now make more macros for formatting your worksheets, and save them in this macro sheet. Save the macro sheet using a suitable name, e.g. FOR-MAT.XLM. Each time you want to record a worksheet, first load this macro sheet. Then activate the macro using the relevant key combination or via a dialog box, which you call up using *Macro - Run*. That dialog window will provide a summary of all the macros in the sheet, including the corresponding key combinations.

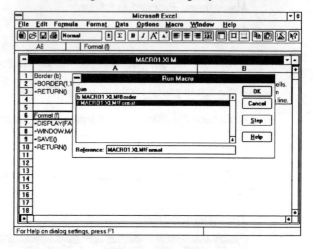

5.3.2   Making a chart with a macro

Task. In exercise 2-2 we entered the quarterly turnover for three regions as external references. We are now going to make a macro which shows these turnover figures as a bar chart.

Apply the following format:

■ Chart title 'Quarterly Turnover': MS Sans Serif 14, bold, border with shadow.
■ Company name 'COMPUWORLD': MS Sans Serif 18, italic, border.
■ Horizontal and vertical gridlines.

■ Border around the chart.

Save the chart as TURNOVER.XLC.

Record the macro. Start the macro recorder using the *Macro - Record* command. Specify 'Quarterly_Turnover' as the name of the macro and a lower case letter q for the key combination. Recording can start:

1   Choose the *Open* command from the *File* menu.

2   From directory C:\EXCEL\EXERCISE choose the TOTWORLD.XLS file.

3   From this worksheet, choose the columns with the region names and the turnover figures (A5:B7).

4   Choose the *New* command from the *File* menu, click on *Chart* and confirm with *OK*.

5   Click on the maximize button for the chart window.

6   Choose the *Attach Text* option from the *Chart* menu, then click on the *Chart Title* and *OK* buttons.

7   Type 'Quarterly Turnover'.

8   Using the *Patterns* command from the *Format* menu, choose a border with shadow for the title and, using the *Font* button, choose MS Sans Serif 14, bold.

9   Add the text 'COMPUWORLD' as unattached text.

10 Choose a border, type style MS Sans Serif 18, italic.

11 Switch on the horizontal and vertical gridlines using the *Gridlines* command from the *Chart* menu.

12 Give the chart a border using *Chart - Select Chart* and *Format - Patterns*.

13 Save the result under the name TURNOVER.XLC, using *File - Save As*.

Switch off the macro recorder now, using the *Stop Recorder* command from the *Macro* menu. Save the macro sheet under the name TURNOVER.XLM.

Exercise 42

Compare your macro with the one in the illustration below:

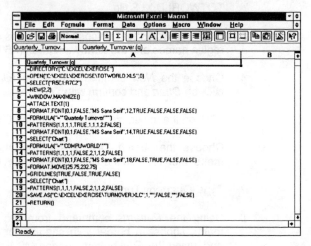

Exercise 43

Start the macro using Ctrl-Q. This bar chart should appear on your screen:

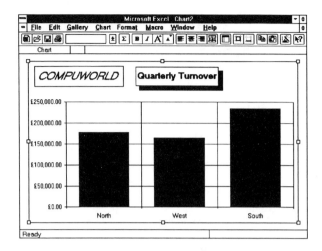

5.4 Custom functions

5.4.1 The structure of a custom function

In contrast to command macros, custom functions cannot be recorded using the macro recorder. This is because custom functions do not perform actions, they carry out calculations. Custom functions can be compared with standard functions. Custom functions require arguments to carry out calculations.

To make a macro sheet for a custom function, choose *File - New - Macro Sheet.* Several custom functions can be put into a macro sheet. You must conform exactly to the macro structure.

First, the macro must have a name. Type the name in the first row of the macro and then choose the *Formula - Define Name* command. In the dialog box which appears on your screen, switch on the *Function* button in the *Macro* box.

The RESULT function is placed underneath the name of the function macro, which is used to define the data type of the function result. The syntax is:

RESULT(data_type)

The function accepts the following arguments:

1   number

2   text

4   logical value

8   reference

16   error value

64   matrix

However, the RESULT function can be omitted. If so, EXCEL uses data type 7. This is the sum of 1, 2 and 4. The result can therefore be a number, text or logical value.

The function arguments are then defined. Every custom function argument must be defined using a separate ARGUMENT formula. Function macros can have a maximum of thirteen arguments. The ARGUMENT syntax is:

ARGUMENT(name,data_type)

The *name* argument is the name of the argument. These names can be used to make the formulas you require for your calculations. The *data_type* can be omitted.

The RETURN function indicates the end of the custom function:

RETURN(reference)

Use *reference* to specify the cell that produces the result of the custom function.

Name the custom function as a function using the
Define Name command from the *Formula* menu (select
the first cell of the custum function on the macro sheet
first).

5.4.2 Using custom functions

To use a custom function, first you must load the macro
sheet in which it has been saved. Only then can you
apply the custom function in a formula. Like EXCEL
standard functions, custom functions can also be included in a worksheet using *Formula - Paste Function*.
Custom functions are given at the bottom of the list,
rather than in alphabetical order.

5.4.3 Example of a custom function

The illustration below shows the PERCENT.XLM macro
sheet with the *Percentage* custom function. This function calculates the percentage of a basic value with respect to a percentage value.

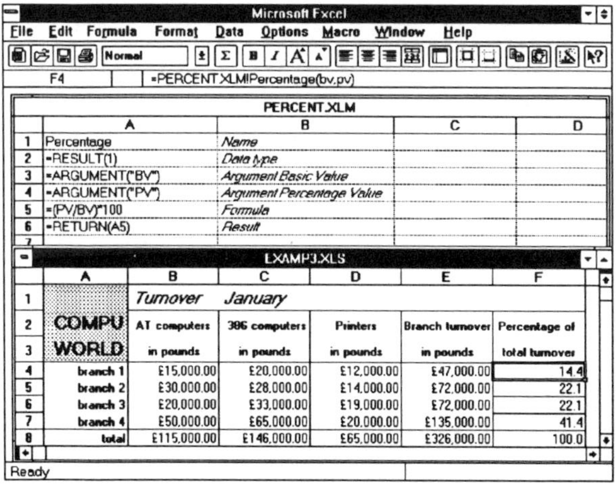

The second row of the macro is used to define the data
type for the result. The arguments for the function, BV
for basic value and PV for percentage value, are in the
third and fourth rows. The formula is in the fifth row. The
sixth row produces the result of the calculation by refer-
ring to cell A5.

We can use this macro to calculate the percentages in
the range F4:F7 of worksheet EXAMP3.XLS. However,
you must first assign the name 'PV' to the range E4:E7
and the name 'BV' to the cell E8.

You can now use the macro in the range F4:F7:

PERCENT.XLM!Percentage(BV,PV)

6 Data exchange

The business community is currently striving to integrate word processing, calculation, data management and graphic data display functions. EXCEL can fulfil these requirements with its Worksheet, Chart and Database program components.

However, EXCEL can also read files written using other programs and can run its own worksheets and charts in other program formats. In addition to these static import and export functions, EXCEL can also communicate with other programs, in other words actively exchange data with other programs. We do not intend to provide an extensive explanation of this dynamic data exchange here, but we do want to show you some of the possibilities of data exchange using several examples. EXCEL's dynamic data exchange does however place high demands on computer hardware, particularly on operating speed and RAM capacity.

6.1 Importing files from other programs

EXCEL automatically recognises the following formats when you open a file: .WKS, .WK1, .WK3, SYLK, ASCII, .DBF, .DIF, .CSV and all EXCEL formats (.XLS, .XLC, .XLM, XLW en .XLT). The meanings of these abbreviations are given in section 2.5.1. If you change the wildcard *.XL* in the enter box of the *File - Open* dialog box into *.*, you will obtain a list of all files in the current directory. EXCEL loads every file, provided it is in one of the above formats.

For example, you may have worked until now with LOTUS 1-2-3, but it is not necessary to re-create all your worksheets if you switch over to EXCEL. You can load the worksheets in EXCEL simply by using *File - Open.* Both the function and the values are imported. The worksheet will work immediately.

The same applies to MULTIPLAN worksheets. However, to import these worksheets perfectly, you do have to save them in SYLK format. EXCEL can also copy most of the format of MULTIPLAN worksheets in SYLK format.

Data from a database can also be imported into EXCEL. If you are working with a spreadsheet or database program which does not support the above formats, it is often possible to save the data as ASCII text and to import this into EXCEL.

6.2   Exporting EXCEL worksheets

Some programs can process EXCEL files directly. In this case, simply load the required worksheet in the corresponding program. You are often also given the opportunity to specify the range you want to load.

However, EXCEL can also export its own worksheets in other program formats. The relevant programs can then process these exported EXCEL files.

6.3   Data exchange between WINDOWS applications

WINDOWS provides a *Clipboard* for data exchange between programs specially designed for this user interface.

The Clipboard is a temporary data storage area. If you cut or copy a selected object in a WINDOWS application (e.g. a text fragment, a series of number values or part of a chart), it goes to the Clipboard.

You can look at the contents of the Clipboard by switching to the Program Manager and clicking on the Clipboard Viewer icon from Main.

If you want to copy the contents of the Clipboard to another program, that program must be loaded. You can
exit EXCEL or refer it to the background by clicking on
the minimize button to switch to the Program Manager.
You can of course do that directly from EXCEL using
the *Switch To* command from the *Control* menu. Start
the required program in the Program Manager. Then
open the desired file. Move the cursor to where you
want to add the EXCEL data and choose the *Paste*
command from the *Edit* menu. The contents of the Clipboard are now copied.

Our next example shows how to include part of an
EXCEL worksheet in a letter written using WRITE.

***At the beginning of every month, COMPUWORLD's
management sends a letter to all its branch mana-
gers, giving a summary of the turnover figures and
notifying them of the branch of the month. Since
the turnover figures are already available as an
EXCEL worksheet (EXAMP3.XLS), these are to be
included in the letter.***

The following illustration shows the part of the worksheet which is to be incorporated into the letter:

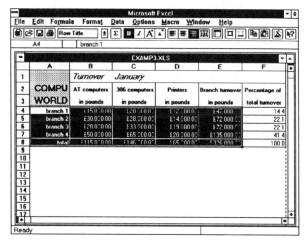

We will assume that the letter has been written in WRITE and that only the figures in the worksheet are missing from the letter. To incorporate the worksheet in the WRITE letter:

1 Select the range A4:E8 in EXCEL worksheet EXAMP3.XLS.

2 Choose the *Edit - Copy* command.

3 Switch to WRITE using the *Switch To* command from the *Control* menu.

4 Move the cursor to where you want to add the worksheet fragment.

5 Choose the *Paste* option from the *Edit* menu.

6 Confirm the dialog box using *OK.*

You could choose the *Paste Link* command instead of the *Paste* command. You will be familiar with this from EXCEL. If you link the worksheet to the letter, changes made to the worksheet will be automatically included in the letter. We will look at this more closely in the next section.

In both cases, the result looks like this in WRITE (see page 213).

To copy data from one program to another, it is a good idea to place the two application windows from different programs alongside each other on the screen.

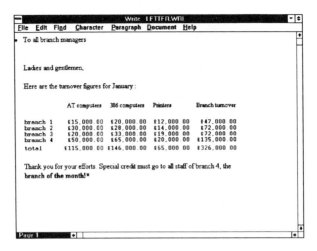

Exercise 44

The right-hand half of the following illustration shows the EXCEL window with the turnover chart. To the left of this is the WRITE window showing the same letter we used earlier.

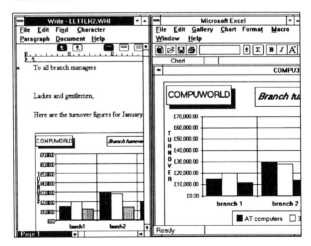

1   Place both application windows next to each other on the screen, as shown in the illustration.

2   We now want to include the bar chart with the relevant data in the letter, instead of the worksheet fragment. Start EXCEL or switch to it and load the COMPU3.XLC chart.

3   Choose the *Select Chart* command from the *Chart* menu and then the *Copy* command from the *Edit* menu.

4   Switch to WRITE by clicking in the left-hand window and move the cursor to where you want to add the chart.

5   Choose the *Paste* command from the *Edit* menu.

6   You can still edit the chart using the *Move Picture* and *Size Picture* commands from the *Edit* menu.

The result on paper looks like this:

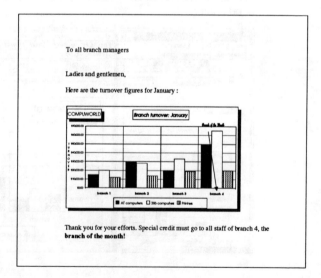

6.4 Object Linking and Embedding (OLE)

Object Linking and Embedding (OLE) offers entirely new prospects. It is possible to exchange data automatically between two or more files within the same application or between different WINDOWS programs.

With OLE, the files whose data are to be exchanged are **linked**. The file/program sending the data is known as the **source** file/program and the file/program requesting the data is the **dependent** file/program.

Almost all WINDOWS programs offer the possibility of linking or embedding files within the corresponding program, for example linking a text file and a number of picture files to a PAGEMAKER publication. Section 2.8.5 describes how to link files within EXCEL. Linking takes place in a similar way in other WINDOWS programs.

Linking or embedding files in different programs is easiest to do using the Microsoft's own WINDOWS program. Simply switch on linking using a button or a check box if you are importing a file from another program or copying part of it from the Clipboard. We used these operations when linking the letter in WORD for WINDOWS to the EXCEL worksheet fragment (see section 6.3).

In other WINDOWS programs, e.g. WordPerfect for WINDOWS, linking to a file from another program requires specific instructions. You have to specify, in a separate dialog box, usually called up using *Link* or a similar command, to which program and then with which file the link is to be made. You must insert a | as a separator between the program and the file.

You can also specify whether the linked data are to be updated automatically or manually. If you choose automatic update, the data changes in the source file are automatically transferred to the dependent file. If you load a file to which another file is linked, the program usually asks if the link has to be updated.

Using EXCEL's macrolanguage, it is possible to start other programs and to transfer commands to them. For example, you can have the following operations implemented automatically using an EXCEL macro: start WORD for WINDOWS, open a document, select a text fragment, copy it to the Clipboard, switch to EXCEL, select a cell and past the text fragment into it.

EXCEL macros can also automatically process stock exchange prices. At a given moment, EXCEL starts a data communication program which requests stock exchange prices via a modem. The data communication program then transfers the price data to EXCEL, where they are incorporated into a worksheet. Once the worksheet has been formatted, a chart of the stock exchange prices is also made.

With Object Linking and Embedding, the macrolanguage and the dialog editor which enable you to make dialog boxes yourself, you will easily be able to develop your own applications.

Appendix A
The Keyboard

The function keys F1 to F12, either alone or in combination with the Shift, Ctrl and Alt special keys, can be used to start commands directly from the keyboard, without having to work through menus and dialog boxes.

This is a summary of the key functions:

F1

F1	Help
Shift-F1	Context-oriented help
Alt-F1	File - New (Chart)
Alt-Shift-F1	File - New (Worksheet)
Alt-Ctrl-F1	File - New (Macro sheet)

F2

F2	Edit
Shift-F2	Cell Note
Ctrl-F2	Window - Show Information
Alt-F2	File - Save As
Alt-Shift-F2	File - Save
Alt-Ctrl-F2	File - Open
Alt-Ctrl-Shift-F2	File - Print

F3

F3	Formula - Paste Name
Shift-F3	Formula - Paste Function
Ctrl-F3	Formula - Define Name
Ctrl-Shift-F3	Formula - Create Names

F4

F4	Formula - Reference
Ctrl-F4	Control Menu - Close (document window)
Alt-F4	Control Menu - Close (application window)

F5

F5	Formula - Goto
Shift-F5	Formula - Find (cell contents)
Ctrl-F5	Control Menu - Previous Format (document window)

F6

F6	Next Pane
Shift-F6	Previous Pane
Ctrl-F6	Next Document Window
Ctrl-Shift-F6	Previous Document Window

F7

F7	Formula - Find (next cell)
Shift-F7	Formula - Find (previous cell)
Ctrl-F7	Control Menu - Move (document window)

F8

F8	Extend Selection (on/off)
Shift-F8	Add
Ctrl-F8	Control Menu - Change Format (document window)

F9

F9	Options - Calculate Now
Shift-F9	Options - Calculate Document

F10

F10	Activate Menu Bar
Ctrl-F10	Control Menu - Full Screen (document window)

F11

F11	File - New (Chart)
Shift-F11	File - New (Worksheet)
Ctrl-F11	File - New (Macro Sheet)

F12

F12	File - Save As
Shift-F12	File - Save
Ctrl-F12	File - Open
Ctrl-Shift-F12	File - Print

Appendix B
The Mouse

EXCEL operations can be carried out using the mouse, as well as using the keyboard. Operations refer to:

- Opening, closing, enlarging, reducing and moving windows.
- Choosing commands, check boxes and buttons from dialog boxes and lists.
- Selecting objects from worksheets and charts.
- Changing objects in charts.

In order to operate EXCEL with a mouse, you must master the following techniques:

technique	description
Point	Place the mouse pointer on a cell or an object.
Press	Press and hold the left mouse button after pointing to a cell or object.
Drag	Move the mouse across the screen while holding down the left mouse button.
Click	Press the left mouse button once.
Double-click	Press the left mouse button twice in quick succession.

Depending on its position on the screen, the shape of the pointer may change. Mouse pointer shapes include:

pointer shape
     screen location
          function

menu bar, scroll bars, chart window
    point or select

formula bar, enter box in dialog box
    inserting at a particular place

worksheet
    selecting cells or ranges

between two rows
    adjusting row height

between two columns
    adjusting column width

in window corner
    resizing window horizontally or vertically

along window border
    resizing window horizontally and vertically

screen divider left of horizontal scroll bar
    dividing window into two vertical panes

screen divider above vertical scroll bar
    dividing window into two horizontal panes

top left-hand corner of the screen (after *Window Menu -
Split* command in document window)
    simultaneously dividing window into two vertical
    and two horizontal panes

on the Sample Page
    magnifying

in the middle of the screen after Shift-F1
    requesting help for the topic you click on next

in the Help window after placing the pointer on a frame
or underlined item
> requesting extra information

 anywhere on the screen during operations
> indicates that an action is underway and that the
> user must wait until new actions are possible

 on a worksheet when copying cell contents by dragging
> release mouse button to copy cell contents

 any area of screen where you need help when you
press Shift+F1
> choose the command or click the area of screen
> on which you want Help

Appendix C
Summary of menu
commands

The options you see in the menu bar depend on the window you are in at the time - worksheet window, chart window, macro window or info window. If no files are loaded, only the basic menu is available. A menu is opened by clicking on its name with the mouse or pressing the Alt key, together with the underlined letter in the menu name.

The menu commands can be chosen in the same way. The ellipsis (...) behind an option means that you can call up a dialog box by clicking on the option. The settings required to carry out the command can then be specified.

Using the *Shortcut Menus*, activated by pressing the right mouse button, you can restrict the menus to the most frequently used commands.

Worksheet window

File

New...	
Open...	Ctrl+F12
Close...	
Links	
Save	Shift+F12
Save As...	F12
Save Workbook...	
Delete...	
Print Preview	
Page Setup...	
Print...	Ctrl+Shift+F12
Print Report...	
Exit	Alt+F4

Edit

Undo	
Repeat	
Cut	Ctrl+X
Copy	Ctrl+C
Paste	Ctrl+V
Clear...	Del
Paste Special...	
Paste Link	
Delete	
Insert	
Insert Object	
Fill Right	
Fill Down	

Formula

Paste Name...	
Paste Function...	
Define Name...	
Create Names...	
Apply Names...	
Note	
Goto...	F5
Find...	Shift+F5
Replace...	
Select Special...	
Show Active Cell	
Outline	
Goal Seek...	
Scenario Manager	
Solver...	

Format

Number...
Alignment...
Font...
Border...
Patterns...
Cell Protection...
Style...
Auto Format
Row Height...

Column Width...
Justify
Bring To Front
Send To Back
Group
Object Properties...

Data

Form...
Find
Extract...
Delete
Set Database
Set Criteria
Set Extract
Sort...
Series...
Table...
Parse...
Consolidate...
Crosstab...

Options

Set Print Area
Set Print Titles
Set Page Break
Display...
Toolbars...
Color Palette...
Protect Document...
Calculation...
Workspace...
Add-ins...
Spelling...
Group Edit...
Analysis Tools...

Macro

Run...
Record...
Start Recorder...
Set Recorder

Rel<u>a</u>tive Record
Assign to <u>O</u>bject...
R<u>e</u>sume

<u>W</u>indow

<u>N</u>ew Window
<u>A</u>rrange...
<u>H</u>ide
<u>U</u>nhide...
<u>V</u>iew...
<u>S</u>plit...
<u>F</u>reeze Panes
<u>Z</u>oom...
<u>1</u>Sheet1

<u>H</u>elp

<u>C</u>ontents...   F1
<u>S</u>earch...
<u>P</u>roduct Support
<u>I</u>ntroducing Microsoft Excel
<u>L</u>earning Microsoft Excel
L<u>o</u>tus 1-2-3...
<u>M</u>ultiplan...
<u>A</u>bout Microsoft Excel...

Chart Window

<u>F</u>ile

<u>N</u>ew...
<u>O</u>pen...   Ctrl+F12
<u>C</u>lose
<u>L</u>inks...
<u>S</u>ave   Shift+F12
Save <u>A</u>s...   F12
Save <u>W</u>orkbook...
<u>D</u>elete...
Print Pre<u>v</u>iew
Page Se<u>t</u>up...
<u>P</u>rint...   Ctrl+Shift+F12
E<u>x</u>it   Alt+F4

Edit

Undo	
Repeat	
Cut	Ctrl+X
Copy	Ctrl+C
Paste	Ctrl+V
Clear	Del
Paste Special...	

Gallery

Area...
Bar...
Column...
Line...
Pie...
Radar
XY (Scatter)...
Combination ...
3-D Area...
3-D Bar...
3-D Column...
3-D Line...
3-D Pie...
3-D Surface...
Preferred
Set Preferred

Chart

Attach Text...
Add Arrow
Add Legend
Axes...
Gridlines
Add Overlay
Edit Series...
Select Chart
Select Plot Area
Protect Document...
Color Palette...
Calculate Now
Spelling...

Format

> Patterns...
> Font...
> Text
> Scale...
> Legend...
> Main Chart...
> Overlay...
> 3-D View...
> Move
> Size

Macro

> Run...
> Record...
> Start Recorder...
> Resume

Window

> Arrange
> Hide
> Unhide...
> 1Chart1

Help

> Contents...   F1
> Search...
> Product Support
> Introducing Microsoft Excel
> Learning Microsoft Excel
> Lotus 1-2-3...
> Multiplan...
> About Microsoft Excel...

Info Window

File

> New...
> Open...
> Close...
> Save Workbook...

Delete...
Print Preview
Page Setup...
Print...
Exit

Info

Cell
Formula
Value
Format
Protection
Names
Precedents...
Dependents...
Note

Macro

Run...
Record...
Start Recorder
Resume

Window

Show Document
Arrange...
Unhide...
1Sheet1

Help

Contents...
Search...
Product Support
Introducing Microsoft Excel
Learning Microsoft Excel
Lotus 1-2-3...
Multiplan...
About Microsoft Excel...

Control Menu Application Window

Restore	
Move	
Size	
Minimize	
Maximize	
Close	Alt-F4
Switch To	Ctrl-Esc
Run...	

Control Menu Document Window

Restore	Ctrl-F5
Move	Ctrl-F7
Size	Ctrl-F8
Minimize	Ctrl-F9
Maximize	Ctrl-F10
Close	Ctrl-F4
Next Window	Ctrl-F6

Appendix D
Error Values

If faults occur during formula calculation, you will see an error value in the relevant cell. An error value always starts with a number sign (#). Below is a list of error values and their possible causes:

error value	cause
#DIV/0!	the formula contains a division by 0
#N/A	no value available
#NAME?	a name has been used which EXCEL does not recognise
#NULL!	a cross section has been specified but the ranges do not cross
#NUM!	problem with a number (e.g. the wrong argument in a function)
#REF!	reference to an invalid cell
#VALUE!	the wrong type of argument or operand has been used

Appendix E
Chart types

This appendix summarises the types of charts available in EXCEL.

Area chart

Types:
1 simple area chart
2 100% area chart
3 area chart with drop lines
4 area chart with gridlines
5 area chart with labelled areas

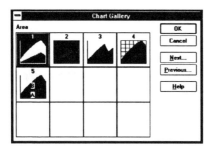

Horizontal bar chart

Types:
1 simple horizontal bar chart
2 horizontal bar chart for one series with varied patterns
3 stacked horizontal bar chart
4 overlapped horizontal bar chart
5 100% stacked horizontal bar chart
6 horizontal bar chart with vertical gridlines
7 horizontal bar chart with value labels
8 horizontal bar chart with no space between categories (step chart)

9 stacked horizontal bar chart with lines connecting data in the same series
10 100% stacked horizontal bar chart with lines connecting data in the same series

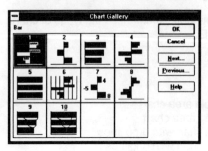

Column chart

Types:
1 simple column chart
2 column chart for one series with varied patterns
3 stacked column chart
4 overlapped column chart
5 100% stacked column chart
6 column chart with horizontal gridlines
7 column chart with value labels
8 column chart with no space between categories (step chart)
9 stacked column chart with lines connecting data in the same series
10 100% stacked column chart with lines connecting data in the same series

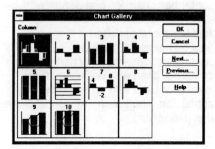

Line chart

Types:

1 lines and data markers
2 lines only
3 data markers only
4 lines and data markers with horizontal gridlines
5 lines and data markers with horizontal and vertical gridlines
6 lines and data markers with logarithmic scale and gridlines
7 hi-lo chart with data markers and hi-lo lines
8 high, low, close chart
9 open, high, low, close chart

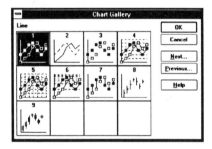

Pie chart

Types:
1 simple pie chart
2 pie chart with one pattern and category labels
3 pie chart with first wedge exploded
4 pie chart with all wedges exploded
5 pie chart with category labels
6 pie chart with value labels expressed as percentages
7 pie chart with category labels and value labels expressed as percentages

Pie charts can only display one series of data. If you select several series, EXCEL only uses the first one.

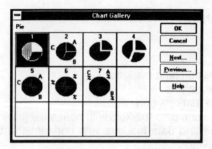

Radar chart

Types:
1 lines connect data markers in the same series
2 lines only
3 lines without axes
4 lines with axes and gridlines
5 lines with axes and logarithmic gridlines

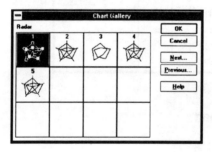

XY (Scatter) chart

Types:
1 data markers only
2 data markers from the same series connected by lines
3 data markers with horizontal and vertical gridlines
4 data markers with semi-logarithmic gridlines
5 data markers with log-log gridlines

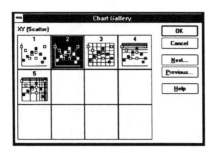

Combination charts

EXCEL divides the data series equally between the main chart and the overlay. If there is an odd number of data series, the main chart will have one extra series.

Types:
1 column chart overlaid by a line chart
2 column chart overlaid by a line chart with an independent y-axis scale
3 line chart overlaid by a line chart with an independent y-axis scale
4 area chart overlaid by a column chart
5 column chart overlaid by a line chart containing three data series
6 column chart overlaid by a line chart containing four data series

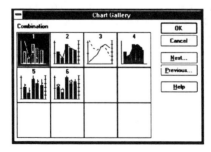

Three-dimensional area charts

Types:
1 simple area chart with 3-D data markers
2 area chart with labelled areas and 3-D data markers
3 area chart with drop lines and 3-D data markers
4 area chart with gridlines and 3-D data markers
5 three-dimensional plot
6 three-dimensional plot with gridlines
7 three-dimensional plot with x-axis and y-axis grid-lines only

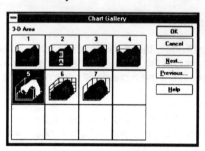

Three-dimensional bar chart

Types:
1 simple bar chart with 3-D data markers
2 stacked bar chart with 3-D data markers
3 100% stacked bar chart with 3-D data markers
4 bar chart with 3-D data markers and gridlines for the value axis (z-axis)

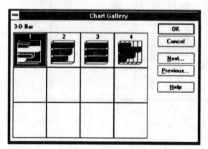

Three-dimensional column chart

Types:
1 simple column chart with 3-D data markers
2 stacked column chart with 3-D data markers
3 100% stacked column chart with 3-D data markers
4 column chart with 3-D data markers and gridlines for the value axis (z-axis)
5 three-dimensional plot column chart
6 three-dimensional plot column chart with gridlines
7 three-dimensional plot column chart with x-axis and y-axis gridlines only

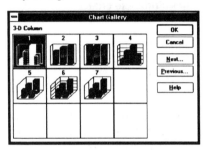

Three-dimensional line chart

Types:
1 three-dimensional plot line chart
2 three-dimensional plot line chart with gridlines
3 three-dimensional plot line chart with x-axis and y-axis gridlines only
4 three-dimensional plot line chart with logarithmic gridlines

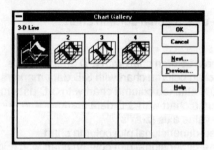

Three-dimensional pie charts

Types:
1 simple three-dimensional pie chart
2 three-dimensional pie chart with one pattern and with category labels
3 three-dimensional pie chart with first wedge exploded
4 three-dimensional pie chart with all wedges exploded
5 three-dimensional pie chart with category labels
6 three-dimensional pie chart with category labels and value labels expressed as percentages

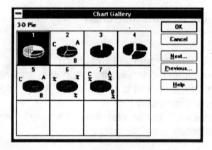

Three-dimensional surface charts

Types:
1 three-dimensional surface chart
2 three-dimensional wireframe chart
3 two-dimensional colour contour chart
4 two-dimensional wireframe contour chart

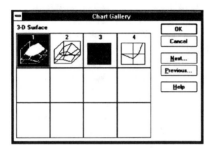

Index

Printed in Great Britain
by Amazon